About the

Geoff Wightman

Geoff Wightman was born in Dartford in 1
Commonwealth Games marathon and 6th in the European Championships
marathon, both in 1990.

He works as Sport Marketing Manager for Puma UK and was the inaugural
head of UK Athletics Road Running Policy and Support Team between 1999
and 2002.

He has been the Flora London Marathon finish line announcer since 1991,
which is a hell of a lot of Batman, pink fairy and ostrich costumes to welcome
home.

He is a life member of Dartford Harriers and lives with his wife Susan and
three children in Surrey.

His debut novel, *Sport Armageddon*, was published by Descartes Publishing
Limited in December 2001.

Dave Bedford

Dave Bedford was born in Hampstead, London in 1949. He still lives there thirty
yards from the maternity hospital where he was born. Since it is now an old
people's home he expects to stay there again one day.

He is a life member of Shaftesbury Barnet Harriers. A colourful career as an
athlete saw him win the International (now World) Cross Country title in 1971,
and culminated in 1973 with a world record for 10,000m on the track at Crystal
Palace. At one time he held every British record from 2000m to 10,000 –
including the steeplechase.

He was responsible for the development of the International Athletes Club
(IAC) in the 70s and 80s and became the inaugural Secretary of the British
Athletic Federation in 1992. He is now the race director of the London Marathon
and in 2003 was elected to the IAAF Cross Country and Road Running Committee.
His son Tom won the English School's senior steeplechase title in 2002.

Dave's moustache was recently awarded protected monument status.

Funny Running Shorts

...101 stories from the world of running

by Geoff Wightman
and Dave Bedford

A CIP catalogue record of this book is available at the British Library

First published in 2003 by Descartes Publishing Limited

ISBN 0 9541718 2 9

Typeset by Mike Taylor; Cover by Karen Johnson; Publisher Liz Birchall
Photography by Mark Shearman – Athletics Images

Dave Bedford photograph – Gerry & Mark Cranham Colour Library

Illustrations by Thomas Mayo Sports Art – www.tommayogallery.com

Printed and bound in Great Britain by Biddles Limited.

Published by Descartes Publishing Limited, 83 Park Road, Peterborough,
Cambridgeshire PE1 2TN

GW:

For Jack, Nancy, Derek and Angela.

DB:

Dedicated to those who have shared the odd beer with me.

Contents

Foreword

Around the world, whenever a group of runners gathers together, often at a race or on a training run, but usually in a bar or a restaurant, the anecdotes start to flow. One such occasion was the Flora London Marathon's 21st birthday dinner, on the eve of the 2001 race (Saturday 21st April). The table that seated Wightman and Bedford also had Steve Jones, Charlie Spedding and the legendary Jim Hogan in cracking form. After the stories had been batted back and forth for some while, Bedford turned to Wightman and said, 'We should write these down you know. We must do a book.'

'We must,' agreed Wightman and a handshake sealed the venture there and then.

More than two years later, and after much trawling, 'Funny Running Shorts' has finally landed. By the way, Duncan Mackay, you're right. There is no rational reason why it should specifically be 101, and not 100 stories. It is just a Dalmatian thing. The ripping yarns format has been wheeled out successfully in rugby, football, golf, cricket and even angling, so now it is running's turn. Runners of all standards are a particularly rich source of amusing stories but, by gum, they sometimes need some prompting. Many times we were referred to someone who, we were assured, would be steeped in rib-tickling recollections, only to be met with a blank stare when his or her favourite story was requested. It would need one of the Authors to launch into half a dozen of their own reminisces and then, somewhere near the end, the pilot light would spark up in their eyes ... 'Chased by a horse in training, you say. That was nothing. I remember the time that ....' And, in true Monty Python fashion, we were away.

Storytelling is definitely a team activity. This book's finest hour was just before Christmas 2002, when a group of Britain's distance running stars from the 60s and 70s gathered for a reunion dinner in London. The output was prodigious, with 20 of those tales making it into this final version. Our grateful thanks to those contributors and everyone else who gave so generously of their wit and memories.

Work has already begun on Funny Running Shorts II, with the first thirty anecdotes in place. If you have a true running story that you would like to submit for consideration, please write to the Authors c/o Descartes Publishing Ltd, 83 Park Road, Peterborough PE1 2TN. All contributions will be acknowledged and receive a free copy of the book.

Particular thanks are due to our vetting panel of Ian Patten, Susan Wightman and Liz Birchall for their help in whittling down 160 anecdotes to the final 101. Liz Birchall, as publisher, has lent the project wisdom and authority beyond her tender years. Thanks are also due to Matthew Fraser Moat and the rest of his team at Descartes, to Mark 'Two from the top please, Carol' Shearman for world-class photography, as always and to Tom Mayo for superb illustrations.

We very much hope that you will enjoy these stories. Keep on running.

GEOFF WIGHTMAN
DAVE BEDFORD
London, November 2003

Contributors to Funny Running Shorts ... and their descriptions

Bill Adcocks	International marathon runner, two times winner in Japan
Jim Alder	Commonwealth and European medallist for 10,000m and marathon
Steve Anders	GB road and cross-country international, 28.26 10,000m runner
Mel Batty	Former 10 mile world record holder – twice national cross-country champion
John Bicourt	Twice Olympic steeplechaser. Former coach and manager of elite athletes
Liz Birchall	Publisher of *Athletics Weekly*
Jack Buckner	Former international 5000m runner
Billy Burns	International Mountain Runner
John Caine	Former international runner (60s-70s), now event organiser with Nova international
Seb Coe	Former Olympic Gold medallist
Malcolm Croft	Co-owner of Tortoise and Hare running specialists
Frank Dick	UK's former chief athletics coach, president of European Athletic Coaches association
Andy Edwards	Journalist, broadcaster and distance runner
Peter Elliott	Former Olympic 1500m silver medallist and Commonwealth 1500m champion
Don Faircloth	Worlds fastest 21-year-old marathon runner in the 1970s
Jo Fenn	GB 800m runner
Chris Finill	GB international ultra runner and London Marathon ever-present
Brendan Foster	Olympic medallist, former world record-holder and founder of the Great North Run
Duncan Gaskell	Finance Partner, Kim McDonald International Management
Nigel Gough	Great North Run organising team
Dave Hart	Great North Run organising team
Lisa Heyes	England and GB international runner ... and very sound sleeper

Peter Hier	Athlete representative and road race organiser
Jim Hogan	International 10,000m runner and European Marathon champion 1966
Syd Hope	North Staffs and City of Stoke road and cross country runner 1964 -74
Bashir Hussain	International distance runner
Tim Hutchings	Former international 5000m runner and current Eurosport commentator
Hugh Jones	Winner of second London Marathon
Mark King	International cross-country runner
Sam Lambourne	2.18 marathon runner, coach and running shop owner
Paul Larkins	Former GB international runner, current editor of *Running Fitness* magazine
Gary Lough	World Championship finalist and European Cup 1500m runner
Duncan Mackay	Athletics correspondent of *The Guardian*
Tom Mayo	Sport Artist
Mike McLeod	Former Olympic medallist and top road runner
David Moorcroft	Chief executive of UK Athletics and former world 5000m record holder
Charlie Mussett	Great North Run finish director
Richard Nerurkar	Former GB international distance runner
Jackie Newton	Former GB and Welsh international
John Nuttall	Sports masseur from Preston
Paul O'Callaghan	Former Irish international, 5000m
Ian Patten	Geoff Wightman's best man and 2.15 marathon runner (with shorts)
Nick Pearson	Former international 800m runner, and senior footwear buyer at Sweatshop
Paula Radcliffe	
Sue Richardson	Ex London marathon 'girl Friday', now marketing co-ordinator for IAAF
Jon Ridgeon	Former 110m hurdles world silver medallist
Chris Robison	Former GB international, renowned for training around a ship's deck!
Nick Rose	Former international 5000m runner and card shark

Sarah Rowell	Former UK marathon record-holder
Allan Rushmer	1968 Olympic 5000m runner and 1966 Commonwealth bronze medallist
Andy Smith	Slow runner and Professor of Exercise and Sports Science
Joyce Smith	1972 and 1984 Olympic runner. Winner of first two London Marathons
Steve Smythe	Athletics writer and reigning GB M45 marathon champion
Ian Stewart	Former racer, now jogger
Angela Tooby-Smith	Former world cross country silver medallist and 1988 Olympian
Nick Troop	Publisher of *Runners World* ... running less than he should.
Bruce Tulloh	Former European 5000m champion
Nigel Walsh	40 something, father of two, husband of one and veteran of 38 marathons
Derek Wightman	"Geoff has been like a brother to me" ...
Susan Wightman (nee Tooby)	First British woman to break 70.00 for a half marathon. 12th in Seoul Olympics
Graham Williamson	3.50 mile runner
Matthew Yates	World championship 1500m finalist

1960S ...

Baggy shorts, cinder tracks,

Knee deep plough, nine mile hacks

Beatle Mania, Parlie Hill

Start your streak, young Ron Hill

Ford Cortina? Non-stop drive ...

Yet to build M25

❖ 1 ❖
JIM ALDER

WHEN the 'International' (now 'World') Cross-Country Championships were held in Rabat, Morocco, Mike Freary, Tim Johnston and I made a shopping trip into one of the local markets. Johnston saw a real scoop purchase on one of the clothing stalls and went for it. When he worked out the currency conversion, he was very proud to discover that he had been able to buy ten pairs of underpants for just under a quid. He went on about it all day and was very impressed with his eye for a bargain. He was slightly less impressed and proud when he unwrapped them back at the hotel and discovered that all ten pairs were equipped with only one leg.

❖ 2 ❖
MEL BATTY

BACK in the 60s, the Rochester 5-mile road race was one of the classiest events in the British winter calendar. It became traditional that if you won this race you would be automatically selected to run for Britain in an international 10k in Barcelona the following month. I was delighted to win but dismayed to find that my team-mates on the trip were all from the North East, including Jimmy Alder. I don't speak any foreign languages but by the end of the weekend, I still felt I could understand our Spanish hosts speaking Spanish better than I could understand my Geordie colleagues English.

❖ 3 ❖
DAVE BEDFORD

WHEN Jim Hogan ran in one of the International cross-country races, which were the forerunner of the World Cross Country Championships, he did not care for the fact that the organiser had included a couple of man-made barriers on each of the laps. He ran around the outside of each and every one of them, blaming the congested approach. When

the results appeared it said 'Hogan, England DQ'. Jim was not happy about this and marched over to the referee.

'Why the feck have you disqualified me?'

'Because you didn't jump any of the hurdles.'

'You show me where in the feckin' rules it says that you have to jump over the hurdles'.

The referee then leafed through the rulebook and read aloud

'Competitors must negotiate all barriers on the course'.

Exactly. I did feckin' negotiate them. I went round them.'

The ultimate irony of this episode is that Jim is now involved in training horses to run in the Cheltenham National Hunt racing festival.

❖ 4 ❖
ALLAN RUSHMER

I HAD quite a bad reputation for not leading in races because I preferred to sit in and kick at the end. I did not realise quite how bad things had become until I got to a track match in Budapest for GB against Hungary, where points, and not times, were all-important. You know those short distance velodrome track cycling events where the bikes balance on the start line with neither rider wanting to make the first move because it's usually the rider behind who slipstreams and then sprints through at the end? Well, in the 5000m in Budapest we had the running equivalent of that. There were only four runners for my race. The starter called us to the line, said 'On your marks' and fired the gun. Nobody moved.

The starter clearly thought we had misunderstood the nature of 'bang' so he had another go. We were told to step back. 'On your marks.' We crouched forward on the line. The gun went. Nobody moved.

This time we were warned that when the gun went the race had to get under way so, very reluctantly, at the third time of asking we all went on our way but at a speed that would have done a zimmer frame user proud ... led by me!

❖ 5 ❖
DAVE BEDFORD

IT remains one of my proudest achievements that in my youth I managed to win both the Southern Senior and Junior Cross-Country Championships on the same day at Parliament Hill. The following year, the organisers switched the timetable around so that it could not realistically be attempted again but that year the senior race, over nine miles, started first. Having won that, I must confess that I lined up for the Junior six miles a few minutes later, for a bit of a lark. It was originally my intention to drop out at the top of the first big hill after the start. When we got to the top of the hill I decided that there were far too many spectators to step off, so I decided to carry on for another half mile. Over that next 800 metres, I started to feel much better and got into a nice rhythm, so I decided that I ought to try and complete the first full three mile lap.

At the end of the lap, somebody called out to me that I was 200 metres clear of second place. I was pretty tired but I thought I would never have an opportunity to pull off a double like this again so I pressed on. At the finish I was over a minute ahead of the second place runner. I was very proud of my day's work and it is still a fond memory. Not everyone was impressed though. A few days later I got a letter from the irate mother of one of the beaten athletes. In it she accused me of showing off and being a big-headed so-an-so who had completely spoiled the Southern Junior race.

♣ 6 ♣
DAVE BEDFORD

JIM HOGAN and I went for a brisk training run around the Teddington area on one occasion. I led across a footbridge, which had a large metal warning sign positioned to one side. As we came off the bridge and down the slope on the far side, Hogan was only a stride behind me. At the last moment I saw the edge of this sign and snapped my head out of the way of it. The speed we were going gave me no time to shout a warning to Jim and he smacked straight into it. He hit it at full pelt right on the middle of his temple. He immediately hit the deck, knocked out. He was completely unconscious and lay motionless for a full two minutes. I started to panic a bit. He was showing no indication that he was reviving or indeed, that he was alive. What the hell was I to do? Then, quite suddenly he came to, sprang to his feet and set off running, leaving me to catch up. As I drew alongside, I asked how he was. 'That feckin' hurt' he confirmed.

'Take it easy, Jim' I cautioned, 'You were out cold for two minutes.'

'I feckin' never was' he replied ' I just tripped over for a moment'

❖ 7 ❖
JIM ALDER

AT the 18-mile point of the Commonwealth Games Marathon in Jamaica in 1966, Bill Adcocks and I suddenly discovered that we had broken clear of the rest of the field. I turned to him "Bill" I said "we've got the gold and silver whatever happens". He agreed and we got on with the serious business of deciding who would get which colour medal. It was a very intense race. It was also a big shock, less than a mile later, to hear the crowd cheering and footsteps closing up behind us. Somebody was flying and maybe my prediction about a one-two for the pair of us was a little premature. I looked back and saw to my amazement that it was our team-mate Bruce Tulloh, who had run for England on the track earlier in the week, and had got up early to come and cheer us on, bless him. But did you ever meet a spectator who could run at five-minute mile pace while shouting his encouragement?

BRUCE TULLOH: It's true I was spinning along pretty fast as I urged on Jim and Bill as the Marathon in Kingston reached its closing stages. It was a brilliant race and I didn't realise that I was going quite so fast as I kept in touch, calling out encouragement, a few yards behind them. It started to get embarrassing when the spectators, thinking I was in the bronze medal position, began roaring their approval. It was time for me to take a detour, get off the race route and try and get across to the stadium to see the finish. I tried to step onto the pavement but the spectators were having none of it and pushed me back onto the road

'You can't drop out now man, you've got a chance to win the race.'

This happened three or four times and I had to stay on the road for a bit longer until there was a convenient gap for me to sneak off.

BILL ADCOCKS: The story of what happened at the end of the Commonwealth Marathon in 1966 has never previously had an airing.

Jimmy Alder was well ahead of me as we approached the stadium but I came onto the track first. So what happened outside the tunnel?

The temperature was way up in the high 80s even though the race had started at 5.30am. All of the pre-event planning had based the predicted finishing time on two and a half hours.

The conditions and the course were really too difficult for a quicker time to be feasible. They had not reckoned on Jim and I running as aggressively as we did and we were somewhere inside 2:22 pace as we entered the final mile. As we approached the stadium, the marshals were not all in place and the spectators making their way into the stadium were milling about all over the concourse. We were both well and truly knackered and we were also unsure of the route onto the track. I had lost sight of Jim and with no clear marking, weaved in and out of the throng and made my way straight to the tunnel. Inside the stadium, down the perimeter cycle bank I went and onto the track for the last 300 yards. No sign of Jim. Had he finished? Obviously not, because with 150 yards to go he came bombing past me ... again ... to go over the line in first position.

People thought I had let him past to make amends for what had gone wrong outside the stadium. That wasn't the case. Jim just had more left in the tank than me. What happened was that we were eight minutes or so quicker than anyone had expected and had messed the timetable right up. Most spectators had not found their seats and the VIP party had only just turned up.

The Duke of Edinburgh, Prince Charles and Princess Anne had arrived at the concourse just before us and, in their enthusiasm, the marshals had left their posts, creating chaos. Jim's team manager had beckoned him to the far end of the concourse, which was probably closer to the correct route. Having lost sight of him, I just headed for the tunnel, which is why I was in front of him when I came onto the track. I still have a photograph of the Royal party making their way up the steps in the stand to the Royal Box as I come out onto the cycle track.

♣ 8 ♣
DON FAIRCLOTH

JIM HOGAN has always been one of the great characters of our sport. Someone once said of him that if you deleted all the expletives in his speech, he would be mute. After a short while you stopped noticing that every alternate word began with 'f'. He and his lovely wife Mary were wonderful hosts to the numerous distance runners who were guests in their home, on almost a daily basis, through the 1960s. There was always a hot meal or tea and cakes to welcome you back after a training run. I remember one occasion when the group of us who used to train from Wimbledon Common's famous Lauriston Cottage called in at their house after a run. Mrs H., as ever, was generously plying us with tea and cakes when suddenly the tea tray slipped from her hands and sent cups skidding across the floor. 'Damn!' she said as we all rushed forward to help retrieve them.

'Oi' said Jim from the other side of the room 'That's quite enough of that feckin' language.'

JIM HOGAN
Oi! You can all feck off!

1970s...

Before the arrival of Ovett and Coe

Seventies running needed 'get up and go'

A special young Brit to get the crowds back

To bring Rock 'n Roll to the world of the track

Zappa moustache, red socks, shaggy curls

No that wasn't Bedford, that was the girls ...

♣ 9 ♣

PETER ELLIOTT

MY introduction to running was a slightly unusual one. I had been mad keen on football, and football only, until I ran in the first year cross country race at my secondary school in Rotherham. I won it and the games master was stood just beyond the finish line "Well done, Elliott. You'll be running for the school in the district championships in two weeks time." I protested that this would be a clash with an important football match. He made it clear that if I did not run for the school in this one big cross country race I could forget about my place in the football team for the rest of the season.

I gave the district championships my best shot. After a mile I had just taken the lead as we approached a schoolboy marshal. "Over the fence, down the bank and left along the road" he shouted. The adrenaline was pumping through me and I sailed over the fence and flew down the bank. As we turned left and headed up the road I glanced anxiously back and realised that I had managed to increase my lead and it was a group of just four or five boys that were leading the chase about 50 metres behind. I put my head down and ran for all I was worth. After a few minutes at this intensity, I was very surprised to see a police car draw alongside my right shoulder "Get in," shouted the policeman. "You must be joking" I replied. "I'm in the middle of a race and I'm in the lead. Those lads back there are in second". He pulled the car up ahead of me and bundled me into the back. As my pursuers caught up, they too were unceremoniously pushed into the back of the police car. We asked him why he had spoiled the race. "You can't run down this road. It's the M1."

♣ 10 ♣

IAN STEWART

WE used to have a very large training group for some of our runs in Birmingham in the 70s. The canal towpaths gave plenty of variety and continuous running even through the most built-up areas. There was one particular section of towpath that became a no-go area for a while. Every time we ran there, this horrible dog would appear. I can't remember what breed it was- I think it was a peculiar white colour and a cross between Alsatian, Rottweiler and wolf. I believe it got onto the towpath through a gap in railings at the back of some scrapyard premises. It was probably a guard dog because it was extremely aggressive, snarling and nipping at the runners, however big the group was. Sticks and stones made no difference to this beast. After a couple of bad incidents and no sign of an owner, we re-scheduled that section of the route so that we passed this particular location on the opposite bank of the canal. The first time we did this, the dog appeared as we approached and began barking itself into a frenzy. We quite enjoyed putting one over on this bugger so a couple of us began jeering and laughing at it. This was a mistake. The dog bared its fangs in our direction, made a horrible squeal and launched itself with a huge leap from the bank. It landed in the middle of the canal and immediately began swimming towards us. There were some good runners in that group but I'm not sure that any of them have ever move quicker than they did for those next two minutes!

✤ 11 ✤
GEOFF WIGHTMAN

THE late Harry Wilson, coach to Steve Ovett, was a rich source of anecdotes and a great raconteur. He told one story about a cross country race in France where he and another coach, whom we shall call 'X', were in charge of a British men's team. After a successful day's racing, the evening festivities centred on the presentation banquet in the local village square, where there was a certain amount of drinking taking place. When the team finally rolled out into the square, tired and emotional, Coach 'X' decided to round off the entertainment with a demonstration of his little-known party piece – lighting his farts.

Unfortunately, weather-wise, it was also a windy night and a number of matches were blown out before they had time to ignite the methane. Almost all of the British team was therefore pressed into service as wind breaks. It conjures up a fine picture of team spirit to see so many hands cupped around the remaining matches. The effort and wait were finally rewarded when, with a resounding whoosh, Coach 'X' sent a jet of flame roaring into the night air.

To much applause and considerable admiration, the team strolled back to their accommodation. The next morning, Coach 'X' was less chipper. He came sheepishly into Harry's room.

'Harry. I'm afraid you're going to have to take me to hospital.'

'Why? What on earth have you done?'

Coach 'X' gingerly dropped his trousers to reveal two very large symmetrical blisters on each buttock.

They got in the car and Harry drove him to hospital. Unfortunately Coach 'X's nether regions were so tender that he was unable to sit down in the car but instead had to crouch in the footwell of the back seat directly behind Harry.

Harry refused to go into the hospital with 'X' on the basis of the embarrassing nature of the injuries sustained and watched with amusement from the car park when a formidable nurse, straight out of the Hattie Jacques role in the 'Carry On' films, appeared at the counter to take details. She began recording particulars in the usual way until he came to explain how the blisters had been caused. Then she flung down the pen and looked at him witheringly ... 'You stupid boy.'

✣ 12 ✣
CHRIS FINILL

WHEN I was a student at Surrey University, I remember one term when I was very much looking forward to attending the Guy's Hospital Nurses Ball. The major downside was that it would involve the financially crippling cost of £25 to hire a formal dinner suit from Moss Bros. This was preying on my mind and the week before the Ball I had still not crossed Moss Bros' threshhold to make my £25 reservation. Instead I headed off with the student cross-country team to the Reigate Priory Relays. Many of our expeditions to races were a very hit-and-miss affair. So it was not a complete surprise to arrive at the start to discover that not only had the race got under way more than five minutes previously but also to find that at that same time, our coach driver was disappearing over the hill, not to return to pick us up for several hours.

With time to kill and only the £5 race entry fee in my pocket, I mooched along to Reigate High Street. One of the first shops I came to was the Oxfam charity shop and I decided to get out of the cold and waste a bit of time in there. On the very first rack as I entered the shop was a brand new dinner suit. I could not believe my eyes. I tried it on. It fitted perfectly. I enquired about the price. 'It's £5, dear' said the lady behind the till.

Still got it. Still fits. That suit was always meant to be mine.

✤ *13* ✤

GEOFF WIGHTMAN

MY Dartford Harriers colleague Mr X was delighted that he and his neighbours would be in charge of one of the drinks stations on the Dartford Half Marathon course. The race is always held in late July or early August and traditionally enjoys hot weather, so the water stops are vital.

X wanted his to be a very slick and spotless operation. He took away two huge black plastic watertubs from the clubhouse store and began the preparations for a world class water station at mile nine. He scoured the tubs clean for maximum hygiene and coached all his neighbours in the art of the perfect drinks cup handover. His attention to detail was well received by the athletes, many of whom were tempted by X's nicely chilled refreshment beverages as they sped past the nine-mile point. Unfortunately 100 metres beyond the nine mile point the smooth passage of the race became heavily punctuated by the sounds of retching runners. X had used bleach to clean the tubs and the taste was still there in each and every mouthful of water that he dispensed.

✤ *14* ✤

JIM ALDER

I REALLY did not want to run in the 1974 European Clubs Cross-Country Championships in Luxembourg. It came only four days after I had won the Morpeth to Newcastle New Year's Day race over 14 miles but my club in Edinburgh wanted me in the team so I reluctantly agreed.

It should have been a four-hour journey down to Heathrow by rail but that is where my problems began. First there was a problem with the engine, then we were fog-bound. I was almost three hours late connecting to the Underground, then the tube train was delayed and I ended up dashing for a taxi at Hounslow. I missed the flight by ten minutes.

Customer services confirmed that there were no further flights that day to Luxembourg. The best that they could offer was a flight to Brussels, about 150 miles away, later in the afternoon. I telephoned the race organiser and explained my alternative arrangements. I also had to get someone to call at Newcastle Airport and pay the £40 fare for the re-arranged flight. There was a fault on the telephone line to home so in the end I called my father in law and he dashed to Newcastle Airport to pay for the ticket.

When I got to Brussels there was no-one waiting for me and it was late by this time so I had to find a guest house and make my own arrangements to go by train to Luxembourg early the next morning. What a day it had been. I took to my bed, hoping that the arrangements would fall into place much better the next day. I was just dozing off when I was rudely awakened by moaning sounds and the bed headboard from the next door room thumping against my wall. Someone was shagging on a Herculean scale. I banged against the wall and shouted my displeasure. To my surprise it was a Geordie voice that replied but it must have shocked him more because there was no more rhythmic gymnastics that night. The damage was done, though and I had a terrible night's sleep.

When I finally, finally made it to my room in Luxembourg the next day, some of the buggers from Gateshead Harriers had prepared a highly entertaining welcome for me. Pinned to the door was a postcard of a prostitute showing her bottom, which they had pinched from a London phone box.

I ran a fairly duff race to finish 5th and was not that keen to find that the post-race meal was a disgusting tasting meat. It was horsemeat, I was advised.

Then when I finally made it to my bed the night after my race, there were two dead pigeons nestling between my sheets. 'You should be grateful to find two birds in your bed' I was told by my cackling team-mates..

I really did not want to do that race.

✣ 15 ✣

GEOFF WIGHTMAN

FOR almost five decades, from the end of the War, Harry May and his wife Eve kept Dartford Harriers going, through good times and bad. They did virtually every voluntary job that any athletics club needs, and a few more besides.

They were well liked by many generations of athletes who passed through the Harriers during those years. They are no longer with us, but the new clubhouse alongside the track has a large clock built into it and instead of numerals around the outside, there are letters, which spell out the names 'HARRY AND EVE'.

It's a beautiful tribute and I feel proud of my club every time I see it. Like most athletics clubs, we always seemed to operate on a shoestring budget and no-one was more conscious of this than Harry. One of his roles was as race starter for home fixtures in Central Park and this was something that he continued to do well into his 80s.

He covered league matches, club championships and open meetings. I can see him now, with his peaked red cap and khaki shorts. When he said 'SET', he used to go up onto his toes. There was one particular senior men's 100 metres race where one of the athletes got a blatant flier but there was no recall gun.

As they were moving off to the next event, the starter's marksman had a quiet word with his colleague.

'Was that not a false start in that last race then, Harry?'

Harry's response was unequivocal.

'I let them go. It costs 15p a shot.'

✤ 16 ✤
DAVE MOORCROFT

BRENDAN FOSTER was my main inspiration when I was trying to break into the British team in the mid-70s. In fact I think he motivated many of the distance runners of that era with his determination and bold tactics. It was therefore quite a privilege for me to room with him at the Commonwealth Games in 1978. That was until I encountered his somewhat unorthodox housekeeping arrangements! We did no laundry for the whole three weeks that we were away, despite training heavily. The official Brendan Foster test for whether your running socks needed to be washed was to throw them against the wall. If they stuck, you should put them out in the pile for washing (presumably at some distant future date!) If they slid down the wall, you should wear them again.

❖ *17* ❖

IAN PATTEN

I HAD a successful time at cross-country running when I was at school. When I was 14, I was one of the favourites to win the Northern Schools Cross-Country Championships at Lyme Park, close to my home, in Cheshire.

Whether it was the pressure of the occasion or just the inexperience of youth, I don't know, but I felt tense throughout the morning and I was pleased, at long last, to go for a warm-up jog just prior to my event. As was customary at bigger cross-country events in those days, there was a cannon, or maroon, which boomed out exactly five minutes before the start.

I was a bag of nerves as I fumbled to take off my tracksuit and it was only as I looked down, to check that I had an all-important number on my singlet, that I noticed with horror, that I wasn't wearing an all-important pair of shorts.

I was mortified. There was no point having a rummage through the bag because I had got changed at home. There was no prospect of finding a spare pair from an innocent bystander in less than three minutes. I was all for pulling out of the race but my father was having none of it.

He decreed that since I had a long singlet on, there would be nothing untoward if I ran round in my underpants. I begged to differ but found myself lining up, ready to face the stuff of Freudian nightmares. I duly ran round the Northern Schools Cross-Country Championships, clad only in my Bill Grundy's and billowing vest. I did not live up to my billing as pre-race favourite.

I did not even finish in the top ten and there are those that say that from that awful day my running style changed completely so that I now have a much lower slung leg action and one of my hands moves across my body in the manner of a footballer defending a free kick.

✤ 18 ✤
IAN STEWART

IN the 70s, the fierce rivalry in racing between all of the top British runners was matched by a great friendship between the majority of us and we used to train together frequently. One time I went down to London to stay with Dave Bedford for a few days. On arrival, he showed me upstairs and I was very honoured to discover that he and his girlfriend had vacated the main bedroom in my favour and moved themselves into the smaller spare room.

'That's very generous of you, Dave.'

'No problem' he replied 'we're happy to vacate. There's something wrong with our bedroom anyway. My girlfriend claims to have seen a ghost on top of the wardrobe three times. This room's haunted.'

✤ 19 ✤
DAVE BEDFORD

IT attracted a lot of attention when I first started experimenting with running 200 miles per week in training but at the time I was keen to explore just how far I could take my limits, even if no-one else had ventured into that sort of territory. Mind you, it can lead to compulsive behaviour traits. I used to start my weekly training log on a Saturday and finish on a Friday because the weekend gave a good start in attacking the mileage.

At the end of my first ever week of my planned 200 miles regime, I climbed, weary but content, into a hot bath on the Friday night. I flicked through my training diary and totted up the last seven day's mileage once again, feeling very pleased with myself. To my horror, it totalled 196 miles. I immediately climbed out of the bath, put on my kit and went straight out for a five mile run. Barmy, I know, but I can tell you, should you ever be tempted to try this at home, that a hot bath is all the more pleasurable when you have got 201 miles under your belt instead of a paltry 196.

✤ 20 ✤

IAN STEWART

I RECALL one training camp at high altitude in Lake Tahoe, USA that was attended by many of the leading British distance runners. We cranked out plenty of miles during our stay there. On one occasion, I went out for an afternoon run with Steve Ovett and Tony Simmons and we covered a huge distance. We were still a long way from home as darkness fell and were keen to get off the forest trails and back onto lit roads. Up ahead we could see a wide highway with excellent lighting. It was in the general direction that we needed and there seemed to be no cars using it so we ran three abreast right down the middle. We had not ventured very far along our new found 'road' when we were startled to hear a booming voice on some hidden tannoy -'Will the three runners who have just come onto Runway One please leave it immediately. There is a plane about to land.'

✤ 21 ✤
GEOFF WIGHTMAN

THE first representative cross-country race I ever did for my school was when I was 12. It was at a local school called Parkwood Hall. Over the years we had quite a lot to do with Parkwood Hall and slowly I worked out that it was not a regular educational establishment. It was 'approved'.

One of my arch-rivals was Roy from Parkwood Hall. He and I contested the Intermediate race at the Dartford Schools Cross-Country Championships in Wilmington. He set off like a man possessed but eventually steadied up. I drew alongside and we ran side by side for a few minutes. We had not seen any marshals for quite a while. It later emerged that the said absent marshals were fifth formers bunking off a games period and they had unilaterally decided to go home at precisely 3.15pm even though our race did not pass their way until 3.30.

We both thought we knew roughly where we were going and continued making all of the turns confidently. We pressed on in this way for quite some while. The race was meant to be 4 miles. When we had been running for 45 minutes and reached the motorway section of the A2, some harsh realities had to be confronted.

"We're lost, Roy" I volunteered. Roy concurred but seemed unwilling to ease the pace so we continued, lost at speed, parallel to the A2. Not long afterwards we saw a road sign for Wilmington. It suggested that by the time we got back there we would have covered slightly more than nine miles in our quest for the Dartford Schools Intermediate Boys Championship.

We passed bus queues of giggling schoolgirls. I called out for directions but Roy powered on with jut-jawed determination. At long last we hit the front entrance of the school where the race started. We then had to pick our way through the buildings to get to the playing fields at the back. Still Roy had the hammer down and was rebuffing any attempt at small talk. In the distance we could see staff from both of our teams pacing about anxiously. As we got nearer, in the twilight, we could see the finish funnel being dismantled, the last of the normal, sensible runners having long since finished. This was all the incentive that Roy, a man on a mission, needed. He sprinted for all he was worth towards the point where the finish line used to be, picked up one of the last remaining flags and ran around it.

'I would have had him, Sir' he shouted to the Parkwood PE teacher.

I was mystified. Roy was now wreathed in smiles. Alongside the finish, I could see some of his team-mates standing glumly under a tree. It transpired that a major betting coup had taken place. A number of the Parkwood boys had bet Roy that he wouldn't beat me and, even though we had gone hopelessly off course and run for about an hour, rendering the result null and void, Roy Boy was off to claim his winnings without further delay.

✣ 22 ✣
TIM HUTCHINGS

ONE of the earliest road races I can ever remember running was the Hog's Back event in Guildford. It has a long history of high quality runners taking part and the one time I ran it, the event was an education to me. There are some skills that are unique to road running and as part of my apprenticeship I was about to receive a master-class exhibition. The race distance was 10 miles and for most of the way I was battling away for a place in the top half dozen. Soon it was just me giving chase to the guy in fifth position but the gap remained locked at 100 yards. It didn't matter whether I put in a surge or tried accelerating uphill or downhill, he remained the same 100 yards in front. I forget now who the runner was, which might be just as well, given what comes next. We had risen to the top of the Hog's Back with just a couple of miles to go. I was still working hard on that same gap, when suddenly our man swung left and leapt into the grass off the carriageway. He was clutching at the top of his shorts and his discomfort was obvious. 'Great!' I thought. 'He's stopping for a dump. I've got him at last.' I then watched in astonishment as he whipped down his shorts, crouched momentarily and then rose again, in one smooth movement (as it were). The shorts were back on and he was back into his running quicker than ever. He had stopped for a number 2 and I had gained less than 20 yards on him! This was a hammer blow and he duly kept his 80 yard advantage right the way to the finish. This was a master craftsman at the peak of his powers ... I felt like breaking into spontaneous applause.

✢ 23 ✢

NICK ROSE

THE World Cross-Country Championships were held at Longchamps race-course, Paris in 1980. I had won the National a few weeks earlier and was part of an England team that was favourite to take the team title. The race was over 12kms and I led for about 11.9kms only to be passed by Craig Virgin of the USA and Orthmann of West Germany in the final run-in. That race took a lot out of me although I did not realise just how much until later in the day. By the time we got to the medal presentation, I was still in singlet and shorts, on a very cold day. Next I spent quite a while on media interviews before finally being dragged off to doping control.

I was absolutely knackered and very dehydrated, it would appear. After ten minutes, I had not been able to produce a urine sample. The supervising doctor decided that I should get some fluids through me to enable me to fill the beaker. Unfortunately, with the stadium almost deserted by now and the whole concourse in darkness, the only thing that they could lay hands on was bottled beer. That suited me fine. The England men's team had won. The disappointment of being nipped to the title was slowly being replaced by some pride in getting two medals and giving my all and I also knew that the other England boys back at the hotel would already be starting to celebrate. The first two bottles slipped down without touching the sides but sadly the doctor remained sample-less. I was encouraged to keep imbibing. The doctor was keen to collect his cc's and depart into the Paris night. Anyone who has drunk alcohol quickly on an empty stomach will have some insight into what happened next. Bottles three and four were equally welcome and rapidly despatched and it was only when bottle five was part drunk that normal service was able to be resumed. By that stage I was more than half drunk myself and I stood gently swaying and glassy-eyed as I acted as middle man between the bottles and the sample beaker.

I think it was possibly the first time that this particular French doping control team had collected a sample from a man singing 'Drink up yer cider, drink up yer cider, for tonight we'll merry be.'

✤ *24* ✤
BRENDAN FOSTER

GATESHEAD Harriers always took the AAA 12-stage road relay at Sutton Park very seriously indeed. One year, all of the pre-race predictions tipped us to have a nailbitingly close battle with Tipton Harriers for the title. I was scheduled to run leg nine for Gateshead and Ian Stewart would go on the same stage for Tipton.

I arrived once the race had got under way, psyched up for what lay ahead. Unfortunately a disaster had befallen Gateshead when our first leg runner, Steve Irvine, had gone lame part way round so, instead of contesting the lead, we were last by a long way after the opening stage. There had been a bit of an enquiry about this and the other team members had reacted in different ways.

One runner had decided he was going to go on strike because we were so far adrift. He had not warmed up and when I saw him he was lounging on the grass in his tracksuit and trainers just a few minutes before the leg five runner was due to arrive. I marched over and he confirmed his intention not to run. I was as mad as hell about this. There was no time for pleasantries. I pointed out in a very direct way that I hadn't eased down in training all week to miss out on a run out of any kind and that if he didn't race, he might find that he would need to walk all the way back to Gateshead because I would not be letting him back on the team bus.

He eventually saw my point of view and was persuaded to put on his racing shoes. Two of us then stood him on the start line and pushed him under way as the incoming runner arrived. He ran surprisingly well in the circumstances. We all got a run out. We all travelled home on the team bus. Happy days.

✣ 25 ✣

SAM LAMBOURNE

WHEN you are low in glycogen at the end of a long run, one of the symptoms is an inability to think and act rationally. In the late seventies, some of us were training for the London to Brighton 53-mile race, which took place in September.

The really heavy-duty training fell in the middle of the summer and it was on one of those hot August Sundays when we tried out a really long run. The group included Steve Fortune and Alex 'Ace' Angeli, who was the publisher of several sports magazines including *Athletics Monthly*, and quite possibly the world's most important person.

We knew this from the memorable occasion when he missed the Zeebrugge ferry to a race on the Continent, and, to our astonishment, the boat, having left the dock and made its way across the harbour, suddenly turned around and returned to the quayside to pick up Alex and his lesser stragglers. To Alex it was quite normal that having 'missed the boat', the captain might have turned it round especially for his benefit.

The training run that we tackled was from Brighton to the Eastbourne old town rock and back along the South Downs Way – about 25 miles each way. We made it back to the outskirts of Brighton, dying of dehydration, sunburn and low glycogen.

As we ran through the back alley 'twittens', with the houses backing on to them, one had its gate open. Alex ran straight in, having seen a watering can standing beside the lawn. He grabbed it with both hands, put his head back, and upended it over his mouth with water cascading all over the place. At this stage the owner of the garden starts shouting at Alex to stop drinking his water. Alex immediately pointed out, equally loudly that we've just run back from Eastbourne – quoting human rights and civil liberties and how dare he deny a thirsty man a drink of water etc.

Finally the man managed to get through to Alex that the watering can had weed killer in it. Alex went mad and gave him a right earful about leaving watering cans lying around in case runners passing might want to drink from them.

As far as I know Alex never suffered any ill effects from this and has since been promoted to M. D. (The World).

✤ 26 ✤
SYD HOPE

I MADE my marathon debut at the Northern Counties championship event in Rotherham in 1975. The course was a fairly intricate one-lap loop and as a lead vehicle, we had a motorbike. Shortly into the race, which I was leading, the motorbike rider informed me that he had a problem with his machine and a cyclist took over as race pilot.

Following the bike rider, we weaved our way left and right through the first 45 minutes. At the nine-mile point, I had a lead of around 45 seconds over second place and was concentrating hard on following the pilot. Quite unexpectedly, he dismounted from his bike and started wheeling it down the side of a house.

'Where are you going?' I shouted (or words to that effect.) This startled him. He had got a puncture and had headed back to his house. He had forgotten all about the fact that I was following him.

He had led me almost a mile off course. I turned to re-trace my steps, cursing. The chasing pack, presumably with some local knowledge, had not strayed from the correct route and I found myself approximately 95 seconds down. Fuelled, I suspect by anger, I did eventually get back past them and won in a time of 2:25.45, which remains my personal best for 27 miles to this day.

✤ 27 ✤

IAN STEWART

WHEN we are at a training camp at altitude in St. Moritz, in the build-up to the Munich Olympics, we had a character seconded to us whom we called 'The Doc'. He was an exercise physiologist, or similar. This was well before the days when sports science support in distance running was in vogue and although he was there for our own benefit, to ensure that our training was helping rather than hindering our Olympic preparations, we weren't as helpful as we might have been to The Doc.

One morning, steeplechaser Andy Holden got back from a light training run to receive the message that The Doc wanted to take a blood sample to make sure that he had not been overdoing it. Andy was on his way to qualifying as a dentist and had some knowledge of medical matters and decided to play a prank on the Doc. He skipped breakfast to keep his blood sugar low, dosed up on aspirin and then spent half an hour blasting up and down a staircase so that his body was awash with lactic acid. Then he composed himself, changed and went calmly to give The Doc his blood sample before leaving on a shopping trip. Half an hour later, The Doc came bursting into our room. 'Where is Holden, where is Holden?' he demanded.

'He's gone down to the track for a hard workout. Why?' We were all in on the gag.

'He must not, he will die. I must stop him!' And with that he set off to commandeer a car from reception and headed to the stadium at breakneck speed to try and prevent Andy from killing himself. He would not have been aware that the King of Lactate was casually browsing round the shops at the time, having outmanoeuvred The Doc at his own game. It was like being back at school really.

1980s...

There was a young runner called Coe

At 800 he could really go

Ovett, by contrast

Ran the mile really fast

Was it 'Swap-Shop' we watched in Moscow?

✣ *28* ✣
DAVE BEDFORD

BY 11 o'clock on the night of 28th March 1981, I had consumed a certain number of beers at The Mad Matter nightclub in Luton. This was not an unusual occurrence in itself because it was a Saturday night and, at the time, I owned the said Mad Hatter nightclub. What was unusual was that, with only a few hours to go before the start, someone had just bet me £250 that I could not complete the following morning's inaugural London Marathon. I had not run at all for twelve months but, through my rose-tinted beer goggles, the bet seemed too good to refuse. I accepted without hesitation and immediately began my preparations.

First I needed an entry for the race. I telephoned Chris Brasher to ask for a race number. His telephone manner suggested that I had perhaps woken him up. His somewhat succinct reply was to the effect that it was too late to get a number but why not run anyway. This seemed an appropriate suggestion and I began my build-up in earnest, turning to a more healthy beverage. I downed four pina coladas. The club closed at 2am but because the clocks went forward to mark the start of British Summer Time, it was already 3am.

I therefore turned my attention to carbo-loading. There was an obvious venue that would enable me to do this in style. I headed for the local curry house. The sign outside said 'The Light of India' but we knew it more affectionately as 'The Shite'. One King Prawn Curry and a pint of lager later (you try getting a pina colada in an Indian restaurant), I was ready for a nap. It was, after all, a quarter to five.

At six o'clock I was awoken by my business partner, Johnny Brookes. He had also agreed to run the race but decided sleep would not be of assistance to him. With the London Marathon starting at 9am we had to make our way to the start.

At eight o'clock we arrived and were ready to roll. I felt in top form and anticipated an easy run of about three hours. The gun set us on our way and I headed out at a comfortable pace. Halfway was reached on schedule (1hr 30m) but quite suddenly it all started to go wrong. The curry consumed earlier that morning was making running a little uncomfortable, regardless of how much Vaseline I used. I started to walk, keeping my legs unnaturally apart, Wyatt Earp style, in order to reduce the chaffing effect. I got to Tower Bridge for the second time in around three hours and found out later that I had been captured by BBC TV, losing the rest of the curry into a drain. Brendan Foster, who was commentating, remarked 'There's Dave Bedford, not looking as fit as we might have expected.'

It took a further 45 painful minutes to get to the finish line. I had arranged that I would meet up with Brooksie at a local pub for a celebration but he was nowhere to be seen. I fell asleep in the corner of the pub and was turfed out at 3 o'clock. I headed back to Luton and took to my bed for two days. When I finally did get up I could hardly walk, such was the stiffness.

Brooksie, it transpired, had stopped at a pub at the 6-mile point, got totally legless and finally got back to Luton two days later. The saddest part of all is that I am still waiting for the £250 to be paid up, a mere 22 years later, because the bloke that made the bet never showed his face in the Mad Hatter again.

✤ 29 ✤
STEVE ANDERS

IN January 1985 I went to Los Angeles for the Superbowl 10k road race as part of a small British team. The event took its name from the other big sports occasion that weekend! Apart from Australia, it was the furthest I ever travelled for a race but I was in good shape, being the reigning UK 10-mile road champion. It was a high quality event and I was looking forward to it.

It was a warm day, on a hilly course, but as we neared the halfway point, on one of the uphill sections, I was still with the leading group of about seven or eight runners and working hard.

We passed one of the wheelchair competitors who had set off ahead of us. He was noticeable because of his racing outfit and chair. Wheelchair racing in the UK was not common in those days. We had only had three London Marathons at this point, so they were not a regular feature in road racing. This guy was certainly not an ordinary sight. He had spray-painted the whole of his machine jet black, he was wearing black leathers and had a dark visor. He certainly looked the business. Having passed him, we crested the hill and then had a downhill sweep on the other side. Racing wheelchairs struggle with the uphill sections but are much quicker than runners going downhill. It was still a surprise though, when, near the foot of the hill our man came whistling past in his jet-black machine, in an aerodynamic crouch position. He either over-estimated his own speed or under-estimated our speed. There was a sharp right hand curve at the foot of the hill and he cut in sharply to take the turn. Unfortunately he had not judged the situation correctly and he cut right across our group, ploughing into the side of the runner on the left hand side. Even more unfortunately, that runner was me. I went down like a bag of spuds with elbows and hands grazed and knees banged up.

Badly bruised on my left side, I got up and managed to complete the race, but the most embarrassing thing of all was returning to the UK and explaining that I had finished in lowly seventh place as a result of being run over by a wheelchair.

✢ *30* ✢
DUNCAN MACKAY

WHEN Zola Budd first came to Britain in the spring of 1984, her chaperones from the *Daily Mail*, who had her under exclusive contract, were very conscious that she was leaving behind an outdoor lifestyle and a love of wild animals. Her home in Bloemfontein was almost like a ranch and she had pet dogs, cats and was particularly fond of the ostriches that lived with them.

They couldn't really match this but did their best, and she was duly installed in a rented cottage in the New Forest so that she had access to open spaces for her running. As the rest of the press pack made strenuous attempts to track her down, she moved a couple of times, eventually ending up in Guildford. Because she had to relocate more than once, the paper didn't feel able to get her a pet that was in keeping with her South African ostriches, so they bought her a budgie. She grew very attached to this bird, which followed her from place to place a few days after Zola herself moved house.

The proprietor of the *Daily Mail* was delighted to receive the news mid-year that Zola's application for a British passport, which had been championed by themselves, had been granted. This would clear the way for her to represent Great Britain at the Olympic Games at the end of the summer. It was such a significant development that he decided he would telephone her himself and record her live response to the news and pass it on to the *Daily Mail* readership the following day.

When Zola took the call, it was clear that there was some disruption at her latest dwelling as her possessions were being delivered at the same time. She was somewhat distracted.

'Zola' he said, ' you have today been granted a British passport. Tell me what your reaction is to this fantastic news?'

There was a pause at the end of the line before a memorable response: 'Oh great, my budgie has just arrived.'

✤ *31* ✤
MARK KING

DOWN in the depths of Cornwall where I train we can get some very misty mornings. One morning I was trying to get a training run done in conditions like this. Fortunately, it was a familiar route across fields and trails and I knew exactly where I was even if visibility was down to a few feet. Unfortunately, my guts were playing up and after a couple of miles I had to look around for somewhere to take an emergency pit-stop.

The thick mist helped because at least I had a bit of privacy for this delicate task. I left the main path and scrambled up a bank to where the perimeter fence was located. I dropped my shorts as I squatted down. George the Tortoise was in the departure lounge, and I was just at the point of no return, when a voice directly above me said 'Alroight, boy, nice morning for it?' It scared the life out of me. It was a farmer leaning on the fence. I had my shorts up and was out of there quicker than Ben Johnson.

✤ 32 ✤
JOHN CAINE

Back in the 80's, at one stage Phil Brown, the 400 metres star, was thinking about moving up to 800 metres. He asked Peter Elliot what the distance was like.

'It's like this' Peter explained 'You know that feeling you get when you're getting near the end of the home straight in a 400, when your legs have turned to water and you've almost had to close your eyes because it hurts so much?'

'Yes,' said Phil.

'When you got so much lactic acid working up your body that you can't even feel your arms?'

'Yes'

When you're working so hard you think you might puke?'

'Yes'

'Well, when you're feeling like that you've got one lap to go.'

✤ 33 ✤
JOHN BICOURT

BACK in the summer of 1976 I was on a pre Olympic distance running camp at altitude in Colorado Springs. One afternoon, Ian Stewart, Jeff Norman and myself were driven to a National Park set up high on a pine covered plateau about seven miles away to go for a long run. It was very hot and still and we were told to be careful, as this was bear country.

After we had been cautiously running for over an hour we were about ready to turn back but we couldn't agree about which was the most direct route back. I thought one direction but Ian and Jeff thought the opposite. So we went our different ways.

Distance runners can be quite stubborn, especially when they are tetchy and tired. I was confident I was going the right way. But I was wrong, very wrong as it turned out. For over two more hours I ran on through uninhabited wilderness along what seemed to be endless trails, sometimes jogging sometimes walking. I was now very thirsty and it was still very hot and quiet. I was becoming more and more anxious.

There was no sign of civilisation at all and I became so lost that I could not even work out how to re-trace my steps and the sun was beginning to set. I decided to continue on one particular sandy track that had obviously been used by vehicles. Suddenly, and very luckily for me, a Park Ranger's jeep appeared, coming towards me. "Where the hell are you going?" he asked as he pulled up.

I told him I was lost and he told me that if I continued on the way I was going there was nothing for the next 30 miles! He then took me about five miles back the way I had come to a kind of outback fire station. The fireman were highly amused when they heard my story. They were great guys and two of them gave me a lift on one of their fire trucks all 25 miles back to the US Airforce academy where our group was based. My colleagues managed to conceal their obvious concern over my five-hour absence very well even though they were about to launch an official search party. In fact they fell about laughing as I eventually arrived home hanging on grimly to the back of a forest ranger's fire engine.

✤ *34* ✤
SUSAN WIGHTMAN

MY twin sister Angela and I were very pleased indeed to get a sponsored car from PGL Adventure, for us to share, in the year leading up to the Seoul Olympics. It was a bit of a moving billboard with 'Tooby Twins ... Going for Gold' and various other understated slogans plastered all over the bodywork. We drove that car to death, up and down the M4 between London and Bristol most weeks.

To Angela fell the distinction of the only prang, when she was driving on her own in slow-moving traffic near the Chiswick flyover. She got out to exchange particulars with the other woman driver who acted distinctly snotty throughout the whole process. After they had both written down all of each others details, the woman looked at our car more closely.

'Huh,' she said, turning on her heel and stalking back to her own vehicle 'It's obviously not even your car.'

✧ 35 ✧
CHRIS FINILL

I HAD a very early mid-life crisis because within the same four week period our first son was born and I turned thirty. I suddenly felt like I was getting very old, weighed down by the dual responsibilities of parenthood and entering my fourth decade. It was a strange feeling, as though life was hurtling on and the years were passing too quickly. My first race after passing these twin milestones was in the depths of winter on an exceptionally muddy cross-country course in North London.

I did my usual warm-up and realised just two minutes before the start that I had no shorts on under my tracksuit trousers. There was nothing for it. I would have to race in my baggy fleece jogpants.

It was a quagmire all the way round and by the third lap my long trousers had become so sodden and heavy that I had to run with one hand on them to keep them up. It was depressing to run so slowly and awkwardly. I felt like an old codger so you can imagine how incensed I felt when, not far from the finish line a young lad shouted 'Go on Grandad' as I passed him.

This was the last straw. After I crossed the line, I turned to walk back towards this callow and cheeky youth to give him a piece of my mind. Who did he think he was calling 'Grandad'? Fortunately, before I got close enough to cuff him, an older gentleman passed me and gave the lad a hug. This really was his Grandad and I had just held him off in a sprint finish.

✣ 36 ✣
FRANK DICK

AT the Commonwealth Games of 1986 in Edinburgh, I was concerned to get my athlete Daley Thompson away from Meadowbank Stadium quickly at the end of the first day of the decathlon. It would be very easy for him to get waylaid by the press, autograph hunters and well wishers and he needed to prepare for the all-important second day.

I rushed out of the stadium and, trying to avoid being killed by passing cars, sprinted (well, almost) across the very busy London Road. Because I was watching the cars, I missed the fact that there was a lamppost on a traffic island, in the middle of the road. 'Dong!' The lights went out. Most people will walk into lampposts, very few take a 30m approach run! My nose was in a right mess!

'That's a hospital job, Frankie. You may have broken that', Daley observed cheerfully. There was nothing for it. I would have to go to casualty. With a handkerchief clamped to my nose, I was taken to Edinburgh Royal Infirmary. Daley insisted he went with me. Stadium officials phoned ahead to explain who he was and who I was, hoping for a quick treatment when we got there. The lady knew who Daley was and promised to meet us on arrival and speed us through check-in, as it were.

Sure enough, when we got to the A & E entrance she was waiting outside for us, but the thought of meeting Daley must have got her a little over-excited because, as she helped me get out of the car, her greeting was, 'Hello Mr Nose, how is your Dick?' Daley was still laughing when I came out of surgery!

✣ 37 ✣
JOHN BICOURT

MIKE BISHOP of Staffordshire Moorlands Harriers was a very gritty road racer who liked to run from the front. For some years, he based himself in France and proved to be highly successful in road races at all distances on the Continent. On the occasion of the Paris half-marathon I was in the press bus at the front of a rather classy international field. Mike and Charlie Spedding were the leading British challengers. Mike hit the front almost immediately and built up a 100 metre lead over the chasing pack by about 5k. Unfortunately he followed the press truck as it went up a flyover.

This was a vehicle-only section of the course and he should have been directed to stay at a lower level. By the time the main group reached the same point, they had either been sent the right way by a marshal or one of them had previous knowledge of the race route. When Bishop finally came back down on the far side of the flyover to ground level, he was almost 300 metres behind the group. He was absolutely furious and ranting quite volubly.

One of the race support cars drew alongside him, thinking he had been injured or there had been some other mishap causing this commotion. The car did not stop but Mike immediately opened the rear passenger door and dived in.

As he did so another runner who happened to be just behind saw his opportunity and tried to get in as well. Mike was having none of it and literally booted him out. He slammed the door and ordered the driver to take him to the front of the field. He gave a cheery wave to an astonished Charlie and co. as the vehicle shot past, then when he got to approximately the distance ahead that he had before the flyover detour, he told the driver to stop, got out, and resumed racing!

He then actually extended his lead to more than 300m by the finish line. The race director, after discussion with the other place runners decided that the result should stand and, for his unorthodox approach to a tricky problem, Mike Bishop deservedly received the substantial first place prize money.

✣ 38 ✣

GEOFF WIGHTMAN

THE first time I met Bill Foster of Blackheath Harriers (now a GB team manager and Loughborough coach) was when we were both in our mid-20s and we were billeted together for a cross-country race in Belgium. When you stay with a local family, it's always a slightly ill-at-ease feeling, especially if neither party can speak the other's language but it helps if you are not on your own. We were allocated to a rather smart chateau not far from the cross-country course on the edge of a huge expanse of open fields. The host family was very pleasant but had two eccentric members. I should mention the dog first. It was a poodle. It was psychotic. Whenever Bill or I made any movement it would start leaping up at us, snarling. The family found this entertaining, although they feigned intervention. Perhaps weren't aware that it was trying each time to nip or claw us in the gonad area. We had an anxious couple of days because the dog never did get out of this disconcerting routine.

The second eccentric was Dad, a ruddy-faced rotund man, who only became truly animated when he got the opportunity to give us a one-hour guided tour of his cactus collection. No ordinary collection, this. It covered, as I recall, three industrial sized greenhouses that occupied the whole of the back garden.

When we first arrived, we sat around in the front room, making polite conversation – Bill and I in fluent English and the family in fluent Flemish. Dad grew tired of this relatively quickly and, as the minutes passed, he slumped further and further down on the settee. Eventually he must have lifted his legs up to give himself the benefit of a fully prone position, because before long the conversation, such as it was, was drowned out by him snoring very loudly, much to his wife's embarrassment.

Eventually it was time for bed and Bill and I were led up the stone-flagged staircase to our rooms, or so we thought. There was actually just the one room, and, to our horror, there was also just the one bed.

After our landlady had left the room, we had a quick conference. The unspoken starting point was that we could not see ourselves sharing a medium sized double bed. So we set to work discreetly dismantling it, with me sleeping on the mattress on the floor and Bill sleeping on the springs.

We were happy with this pragmatic solution to an awkward social issue but our difficulties were not over because something else became immediately obvious. The room was absolutely freezing. There were wooden shutters in place but they seemed inadequate against the howling gale straight from the North Sea that was rattling them.

We started with two layers of clothing but even this was not enough. I was the first to don tracksuit and socks but could still feel the cold. When Bill finally conceded defeat and put on waterproofs, hat and gloves, we both started giggling uncontrollably. We couldn't stop ourselves, even when we heard Dad going to bed across the landing outside. I bet he wondered what was going on in the luxurious double-bedded guest suite. We actually wore less layers to warm up for the race the next day.

✤ 39 ✤
PETER ELLIOTT

AT the Rome World Athletics Championships in 1987, I had not been favoured to do particularly well. I had only qualified from the 800m semi-final on a photo finish so it was a very big moment for me to take the silver medal.

I went out for a quiet celebration that evening but was conscious that my room-mate, Adrian Passey, would be running in his international championship debut in the first round of the 1500 metres the following day and I did not want to disturb his preparations. I crept back quietly into our room at a reasonable hour. It was already in darkness and I was pleased to hear that he was fast asleep. I knew that I would not be able to get to sleep very quickly because my mind was still buzzing, playing through the final in my memory, imagining what my future races might hold. I wanted to shout, sing and talk it all through but instead I lay quietly in my bed, eyes wide open, staring at the ceiling. I literally spent the whole night like this until the first light of dawn started to creep in through the curtains.

The room started to brighten up and I looked across at the other bed where Passey was still sleeping soundly. Adrian is a blond, cherubic looking chap, so it was a surprise, to say the least, to find that snoring deeply in his bed was a dark-haired bearded man. I sat bolt upright. "Who the hell are you?"

Beard man sat bolt upright as well. He extended a handshake. "Morning Peter. I'm Bud Baldaro, Adrian Passey's coach. He and I swapped rooms yesterday evening so that he could get a good night's sleep in case you were out late celebrating."

✤ *40* ✤
MIKE MCLEOD

I AM sorry to say that it is still the juvenile practical jokes that amuse me when I reflect on past overseas trips. On one stay in Israel for the Hapoel Games, the British team was billeted in a kibbutz just outside Tel Aviv. I was rooming with my wife who was expecting our eldest son and in the room across the corridor were hurdler Shirley Strong and 1500m runner, Mary Stewart. There were lizards running around out in the compound, which was heavily fortified with armed guards, razor wire and dogs.

When we tried to pick up a couple of lizards, they shed their tails, which is something I had read about. We eventually managed to capture three intact and some of the lads and I thought that Mary or Shirley would love to get acquainted with the little fellows. They had gone out for the evening but by removing the air vent to their room, we were able to get in. We put one lizard carefully in Mary's bed, one in Shirley's and one in Shirley's kit bag for discovery the next day.

There is an art to stowing a sand lizard in a made bed and should you ever need to undertake such an exercise, be sure to tuck the corners of the sheets and blanket in nice and tight otherwise they can get out, OK?

About an hour later, we heard them arrive back in their room. Then it was about a further twenty minutes before Mary retired to bed. That was when the squeals started. We were laughing like drains although we weren't expecting that they would scream so loud and long that the armed guards would come running in.

All went quiet until a bit later when Shirley discovered her own little lodger ... cue squeals once again.

✤ *41* ✤

SUSAN WIGHTMAN (nee TOOBY)

IN my twenties, I had the chance to race on the roads in America several times a year. This fitted in quite neatly with school holidays and, during my probationary year as a teacher, I also managed to get clearance for a leave of absence to race three times on a short trip in November. The races went well and after the third one, I discovered that I had scored enough points to qualify for the Scholls/ARRA Grand Prix Final race that was to be held the following weekend in Hawaii. It was a fantastic opportunity, but it was with some trepidation that I rang my Headmaster back in Bristol to see if he would approve a one week extension to my leave. He was not best pleased and although he eventually did give permission, he made it clear, in no uncertain terms, that whatever happened I had to be back in school in good time for Monday morning registration.

Immediately after the race I began the long journey back home and I finally arrived back in Bristol, more jet-lagged than I can ever remember, at tea-time on the Sunday afternoon. I made a telephone call to a staff colleague to arrange for them to pick me up by car on the Gloucester Road the following morning at eight o'clock sharp. By six o'clock, I could not stay awake any longer and, having set my alarm for 7.30am, I fell into a deep sleep. When I finally stirred I looked at the clock and was mortified to see that it was ten to eight. I must have slept right through the alarm!

Frantically, I rushed around the house gathering my things together and sprinted out the door. I arrived on the corner of Gloucester Road, breathless and flustered, at precisely eight o'clock. Then I waited. It was absolutely freezing and by 8.15, fearing the wrath of the Head, I began thinking of alternative ways that I could get in on time. First, I needed to telephone my colleague to make sure nothing untoward had happened. I ran to the telephone box. As I did so, I had a feeling of unease. With hindsight, an open fish-and-chip shop and a closed newsagents should have been a strong clue. I flagged down a passer-by.

'Excuse me, can you tell me whether it's eight o'clock in the morning or eight o'clock at night, please?'

The lady looked at me as if I was utterly barking.

'It's eight o'clock on Sunday night,' she replied, hurrying to get away from the red-eyed mad woman. I had been asleep for less than two hours.

✦ 42 ✦
PETER ELLIOTT

IN the late 80s, not long after I had won my Olympic silver medal, I was walking back home to my house one lunchtime, after just popping out to the shops. A few yards ahead of me on the pavement a little girl was walking with her mother. As I got nearer, the little girl looked round and said, "We're going to get Peter Elliott's autograph."

"Are you?" I said with a smile

"Yes. He lives in this road" she replied

"I believe he does."

She pointed just up ahead "That's Peter Elliott's house, there,"

" You're right. It is."

We both turned into the driveway of my house together. This puzzled her. She looked up at me thoughtfully "Oh," she said " Are you going to get his autograph as well?"

✤ *43* ✤
SEB COE

SOMETIMES training facilities at major track championships have to be shared between numerous teams. The situation is much better these days but back in 1986 at the European Athletics Championships, the British team would go by coach en masse to a distant training track for a pre-booked session.

On one occasion, our German coach driver got us hopelessly lost and had still not found the track after two hours of driving around in circles. I was team captain and was sitting near the front of the bus. I was becoming very frustrated at the situation and was less than complimentary about the navigation. The driver, who clearly understood, promptly stormed off the bus, muttering under his breath. I noticed that he had left the keys in the ignition. The team was anxious to get some training in. We were two hours late. Fangio had abandoned his post. What is a team captain to do in that situation?

I slipped into the driver's seat, started up the engine and eased through the gears, pointing the bus in what I felt sure was the general direction of the training venue. I had no previous experience of piloting coaches even as an avid viewer of the classic 'On The Buses'.

As the coach arrived at the track I could see a fleet of green and white police cars waiting for us and Daley Thompson, sensing that there might be one or two repercussions, made his contribution to the situation by taking the bus keys out of my hand and hiding them in Head Coach Frank Dick's bag, blaming him for the hijack.

Later that day I was severely reprimanded for my actions and was advised that I had come very close to being ordered home from the Championships.

We thought we might have kept the episode under wraps but the following day at a press conference, I was asked by a grinning British journalist if I would like to comment on the quality of team transportation in Stuttgart. I politely declined.

✤ *44* ✤
GEOFF WIGHTMAN

I TRAVELLED to a big cross-country meeting in Belgium some years ago with my Dartford Harriers clubmate, Gary Arthey and his father Keith. At the prize presentation after the race, I discovered that, once again, I was the first finisher not to win money. The top six Senior Men trooped up and collected manila envelopes but when my name was called, for 7th place, the envelopes had run out. The race organiser explained that I could have first choice from all of the prizes that were spread across the stage. There were cases of wine, whole cheeses, large continental sausages, footballs, picnic baskets, bicycle pumps, boxes of chocolates, hose reels, china dolls, towels, handkerchiefs and fruit. Yes, I believe there was even a cuddly toy. It was an overwhelming selection of probably 100 or more items but the race organiser had a presentation to get through and I had a life to lead so I couldn't spend forever rummaging through his Aladdin's Grotto.

I asked him what he thought his best prize was. He immediately pointed to the floor in front of the stage where there was a rolled up carpet. I had not even realised that this was part of his selection box but took his advice and dragged the carpet off. I was assured that it was a high class Persian rug, with tasselled edges, that would grace any room. It was about 16 feet wide. I felt sure that I was the envy of the rest of the room. I also felt very smug because surely this little beauty was of a much higher value than many of the cash prizes that had eluded me? The other British runners stroked the luxuriant pile of the carpet and murmured approvingly about its quality. There was just one figure who looked a little nonplussed. Keith Arthey. In my haste to snap up the most expensive prize, I had overlooked the fact that we still had to travel back from Belgium to Kent in Keith's admittedly nippy, but not exactly removal van-proportioned, VW Golf.

After much manoeuvring and puffing we finally managed to wedge the rolled up carpet behind the gearstick with the back end sticking some way out of one of the rear passenger windows. I remain very grateful to Keith for making the long journey back with the winter wind howling in through the rear passenger window. The high class Persian rug then remained in my parents' attic for the next 15 years.

✧ *45* ✧
DAVE MOORCROFT

I KNEW throughout my warm-up for the Olympic 5000m Final in Los Angeles that the injury that I had been carrying was not going to let me run freely in the race. As we got under way it was very bad news. The pace was quick and found me out straight away. After a couple of laps I was off the back. By halfway, I was almost 100 metres behind Said Aouita and the leading group. For the second half of the race my pre-occupation was in keeping going and avoiding the ignominy of being lapped. The Coliseum Stadium was packed to capacity but I felt very sorry for myself. It was all a far cry from two summers previously, when I had broken the World Record for this distance in Oslo. This was a disaster, a tragedy, I thought to myself as I toiled round those last few laps. Actually it was nothing of the sort, because in life, sporting endeavour brings nothing that could genuinely be called a disaster. That happens in other walks of life.

This was just a bad day for me personally and it certainly did feel terrible as I walked away from the track for what would prove to be my last Olympic appearance. I trudged out and through the warm-down area and eventually met up with my wife Linda and our young son Paul, who would have been three years old at the time. It was one of his first visits to a track meeting and he was just pleased to see his dad and I was pleased to see both of them. Paul would not have appreciated how crestfallen I was feeling. His first comment did have the effect of making me laugh and restoring a sense of perspective on the occasion 'Daddy, why wouldn't all those other men run with you?'

✣ *46* ✣
JACK BUCKNER

MY best years for running were 1986 to 1989, when I won medals at European, Commonwealth and World Championship level over 5000 metres. Towards the end of this time I was very pleased to be nominated as a representative on the prestigious International Amateur Athletics Federation (IAAF) Athletes' Commission. The IAAF has come a long way in recent years but in those days it was presided over by the late Primo Nebiolo, who re-defined the word 'autocratic' and was not one for consensus or consultation in his operations.

I knew a little of his reputation in such matters but went in with an idealistic approach, keen to try and improve the environment and opportunities for international athletes.

After 18 months of attending meetings and contributing on as many of the issues as I could, I felt that I had a clear idea of how some radical changes could be introduced to take things forward. I decided to put my ideas in writing, and wrote to Nebiolo, at some length, with my various suggestions.

A few weeks passed and I received his response:

Dear Jack

Thank you for your recent letter. I read with interest your various ideas on how the IAAF can make changes for the benefit of the athlete community. It was good of you to take the trouble to consider such things.

As you probably know, appointments to the Athletes Commission are not permanent in nature and your term is now drawing to a close. I would like to thank you for your time on the Commission and wish you all the best for the future.

Yours sincerely

Dr. Primo Nebiolo

IAAF President

✣ 47 ✣

DEREK WIGHTMAN

THE IAC Cross-Country at Crystal Palace in December was one of the major televised races of the winter. Unfortunately, one year they were beset by very heavy snow in the 24 hours before the race and anyone travelling any distance on the day of the race had no chance of getting to South London. BBC television cameras were already there and, with the rest of that day's racing and rugby wiped out, they were determined to go ahead with the race even though only 30 or so runners had made it. In anticipation of this, my brother Geoff and I travelled the short distance from our home in Dartford to see if it was possible to get into the race. I was there to spectate but I must have looked plausible because I was offered a place as well. I was only 17 but it was too good an opportunity to miss so we set off to warm up together. Shortly before the race, we did a few sprints across the snow. Most other athletes were doing the same.

We were alongside one of the area's best distance runners at the time (who shall remain anonymous) and every time he set off on a stride-out I set off just behind him and surged past. He made his sprints slightly longer and faster so I made a point of going just that little bit further and quite a lot faster, all without making eye contact. Then it was time to stretch. I was over six feet tall and quite good at flexibility work so I did the same exercises next to him but each time with an extra flourish. Then it was time for a couple more full out sprints. This time I was really flying. I could see him thinking 'This guy is either a star or a complete arse.'

We lined up as the television cameras panned across the start and I stood directly behind the afore-mentioned runner, bouncing up and down. I was the only one who noticed another camera passing behind the starter and gave a nonchalant smile. When the gun went I set off at some speed, not quite with the leaders, but well ahead of meladdo.

By the end of the first lap, I had completely shot my bolt and to save embarrassment, I stepped off the course and out of the race. I did this quite smartly, completely unseen by my new arch-rival. Thus it was that I was fully recovered and in my tracksuit when the rest of the field finished. I walked alongside the funnel as I spotted my man finishing. Because of the heavy conditions he was in some distress but I extended a hand 'Well run mate.'

He was bent double but looked up and then retched. He was astonished that I had finished so long before him. To complete my day, there was a mistake in the results, as they appeared in *Athletics Weekly*, with Geoff being listed as 11th and myself, Derek Wightman of Dartford Harriers, apparently finishing in 12th place. I hope Mr Speedy picked up on that. It was my best ever 'result'.

Right: Disco Dave's early attempts at sprinting were not a complete success

Below: After the unfortunate episode when he was unseated in the parade ring at Ascot, Nobby the jockey found the racehorse owners started directing him towards their less thoroughbred mounts

Maisie reacted immediately when she spotted her missing earring

Above: Wavey Davey loved it when everyone else joined in

Left: Darth hated it when his main costume and light sabre had to go in for servicing

Right: There were times when Archie regretted adding John Cleese to his coaching team

Below: Maisie was furious to discover that it wasn't her earring

Left: Gervaise and Tarquin had their little tiffs but always got back together again in the end

Below: Despite their smiles, the weight watchers all knew that their blue lunchboxes would contain just a single fondant fancy, yet again

Sometimes Beryl went straight to races from her job as a snooker referee

An irate Barney Bullethead chases after his barber

The woman down the market had assured Ethel that it was genuine herbal shampoo

Above: Try as he might, Billy Bouffant just could not get past Trevor the spot welder

Right: At the peak of her powers, Beryl Potter didn't even need to reach out – she could just levitate a bottle right off the table

Stuntman Stanley found that unless it's the
tenth day of Christmas, you can only ever
get one Lord-a-leaping

Right: Steve Prefontaine

✣ *48* ✣

JON RIDGEON

I WAS still at school when I was selected for my first senior GB international match at 110 metre hurdles. It was a three-way international held in Yugoslavia. I was so excited about it that I just couldn't wait for the race. In sports psychology parlance, I probably became over-excited in the build-up to the race.

At the time, I felt it was very important to be a bit edgy and this was confirmed when I got the lane draw for our race. I was in lane 8. It was a high quality line-up that included my arch rival Colin Jackson, two lanes inside me. The start was going to be so crucial and I twitched around as we waited to be called to our marks. I got away to a brilliant first-time start and was the first to rise at hurdle one. It was important not to relinquish that early advantage and I could sense that as I cleared hurdles two and three I was still ahead, with nobody making a move across from my left.

By this point I was into my rhythm and I attacked every barrier. I clattered a couple of the later hurdles but I didn't lose any momentum. In sprint hurdling, you know exactly how many strides it is from the last barrier to the line and I flung myself forward, dipping really low. I could detect, out of the corner of my eye, that I had not been caught and I punched the air with delight – I had won on my senior international debut! I was ready to celebrate. The large crowd in the stadium however did not seem to be greeting my triumph too enthusiastically and I turned to shake hands with the runner-up.

To my horror however, there was no-one there. I looked back and to my dismay saw all seven other competitors stood back at the start line. It had been a false start and everyone had heard the recall gun except me. I had been so fired up I had run the entire race on my own. I walked very slowly and sheepishly back past all the hurdles to the start line.

Sure enough I did not win the re-started race.

✤ 49 ✤
ANGELA TOOBY-SMITH

DURING the 1980s when my sister and I were running internationally, I was quite injury-prone and used to have to spend weeks at a time cross-training in order to maintain my fitness while the injury was treated. In those days, one non-weight-bearing exercise that was particularly good for cardiovascular fitness was 'running' in deep water. So, most mornings, as soon as Thornbury Leisure Centre, to the north of Bristol, opened its doors, I was in one corner of the diving pool, running as hard as I could. While it provided a good workout, it was a mind-numbing activity and I got very bored hacking up and down the side of the pool. One morning, proceedings were considerably enlivened by an episode which most men who have heard about it claim could not possibly have been an accident.

The pool was quite full and I had been running in the water for about 30 minutes when a man sauntered in, from the male changing rooms, via the footbath. He was directly above me and was strolling along the side of the pool, without a care in the world, swinging his goggles. I couldn't believe my eyes and nor could either of the lifeguards. After a moment's hesitation, one called out to him and the other blew their whistle. He carried on walking while they pointed to his middle. He looked down and then apparently realised what the fuss was about. He wasn't wearing any trunks! He sprinted back to the changing rooms and re-emerged a couple of minutes later, properly attired. I think I'd have got my coat.

✤ 50 ✤
GEOFF WIGHTMAN

ZOLA BUDD ran her first ever race outside South Africa in April 1984. Somewhat surprisingly it was as a guest in the Southern Women's League at Central Park, Dartford, home of the legendary Dartford Harriers. She was under contract to the *Daily Mail* at the time and was kept at a secret hideaway in the New Forest. For the preceding fortnight, she had been feted in the *Mail* as the new superstar in British athletics, even though her citizenship application and place in the LA Olympic team were still some weeks away. That weekend's Southern League drew a crowd of around 8,000 people. Zola's race was shown live on BBC *Grandstand* and film crews from NBC and Japan and around 50 press representatives were also present.

There was an anti-apartheid security issue and we had spent most of the Friday putting in place arrangements to make sure everything went smoothly. My mother Nancy was Dartford Harriers Club President at the time and I was due to do the announcing at the event so we met with John Bryant, Deputy Editor of the *Mail* and his colleague. Zola would warm up for her 3000-metre race at Dartford PE College about a mile from the Park. She would be driven between the two, just a few minutes before the race start.

We had rung ahead to the College to get permission for Zola to warm-up there and they also very kindly agreed to open the toilets and changing rooms in the Sports Hall for her use. We stopped by to speak to the Groundsman and Bursar to confirm details and thank them for this. We were in a large Mercedes with tinted glass windows, driven by the *Daily Mail*. My mother and I were in the back seat. Another lady came out of the administration block to join her two colleagues who were speaking to John Bryant through the half open front passenger window. She was paying no attention to what John was saying but peering over his shoulder and waving to us in the back. I was mystified. She continued with this and was nudging her colleague and pointing at me. Suddenly the penny dropped. At the time, I was a juvenile 23, quite thin in the face, dark haired and wearing big owl glasses.

'Oh my God' I whispered to my mother out of the corner of my mouth 'She thinks I'm Zola Budd.'

I put my hand across my face as I started chuckling. This served only to reinforce her impression that I was indeed the shy South African waif, about whom so much had been written. They both waved at me again. These folk wanted to be the first to claim a sighting of Zola on UK soil and I am sure that is what they told their families after we sped off with the mysterious figure in the back, head bowed, quietly rocking with laughter.

✤ 51 ✤

SARAH ROWELL

IN 1985, I was one of the Dartford Harriers trio who won the women's team event at the London Marathon. It was a memorable day all-round because Ingrid Kristiansen won in 2:21, which stood as the world best until a couple of years ago, and the next two home were me and my team-mate Sally-Ann Hales, both in 2:28, both inside the previous British best. Although we both ran for Dartford, Sally was a medical student in Sheffield and I was based in Eastbourne, so we did not see each other very often. In fact, I can only remember us training together once, when I was visiting my brother who was also studying in Sheffield. It was the weekend after the London Marathon that year so we were both very fit and had arranged to go for a long, slow conversational Sunday morning run over the moors.

Not far into the route, a lone male club runner breezed past us. I can't remember what it was that irritated us – perhaps something that he said in passing or that he kept looking back after he had gone by. Maybe we were just feeling a little competitive. Sally was only six and a half stone, I was about seven stone and our combined height would be about 10 foot 4 inches so he would have marked us down as a couple of girly joggers as he passed us.

There was only one loop back to the residential areas from where we were, so we gave him a fifty yard lead and then decided to track him all the way back. Initially he had put on a spurt to take himself past and was a bit disconcerted to see that we were still only fifty yards back. For the next twenty minutes, his running style became more and more ragged as he desperately tried to drop us. It was particularly entertaining to see how he would manage a furtive look over his shoulder pretending not be checking where we were. From there on as we hit the rough terrain, which Sally and I really enjoyed, he kept applying more and more pace. I hope he couldn't hear us giggling.

After almost an hour, I would guess he was at his maximum race pace and we were stride for stride fifty yards behind. There is something about the male ego that meant he would rather die than drop back or let us re-pass him. Eventually he could take it no more and he veered off the trail trying to look like he knew where he was going but all three of us knew he was turning down a dead end. We slowed to look down the path as we passed and my last glimpse was of him hanging over a fence.

❖ *52* ❖
GEOFF WIGHTMAN

JOHN CAMPBELL is a veteran runner from New Zealand, who is best known for setting a world masters best (M40) for the marathon, running 2:11 in 1990. Prior to that he settled in Kent, immediately after the Edinburgh Commonwealth Games of 1986, and joined our club, Dartford Harriers. As an overseas national, he had to serve a three month waiting period before he could compete.

In the two years that he was with us, many legends and myths were generated by his spartan 'work-all-night-in-a-chip-shop-survive-on-ice-cream-but-still-run-180-miles-a-week' regime. The first clue we had that he was something out of the ordinary was when the race referee gave him permission to run as a guest in the Dartford Road Relays. The deal was that he could run the second leg of the relay but only if he set off after the last of the first leg runners came in.

John had already trained in the morning and had run at least one lap of the course as warm-up. He paced around the changeover area, watching the second leg leaders set off. He was wearing a bulky orange waterproof cagoule, probably a remnant of his sea-fishing days, and we assumed he would discard this. Wrong. After the first 15 runners or so had gone, he suddenly set off after them, still wearing the Bat Cape. He went tearing off.

Up ahead were some great runners from Invicta AC, Blackheath Harriers and Tonbridge. Heading them all was Keith Penny of Cambridge Harriers. Keith was almost unbeatable on the roads in those days and relays were a particular speciality of his.

As he poured on the pace and extended his lead over a top class line-up, you can imagine that he would feel nonplussed to hear the swish-swish of a waterproof cloak getting closer and closer behind him.

'How you doin'?' asked Campbell as he drew alongside.

Keith's reply is not recorded for posterity and Campbell surged past. Less than a mile later, he stopped and jogged back to Keith.

'I don't know this course so I'll run with you if that's OK'

By this stage, Penny was probably beyond reason. He was operating at course record pace and, for the remainder of the lap, he had the swish-swish of the stranger in the poncho, running stride for stride with him. That is, until the final loop of some playing fields, when Campbell got his bearings and shot off ahead again.

At the finish, when Keith had recovered, he looked around for the mystery caped crusader, but there was no sign. Campbell had carried on running, straight through the finish funnel and out for another two 'warm-down' laps.

✧ *53* ✧
GRAHAM WILLIAMSON

IN the 70s and 80s there were many more small team invitations to cross-country and road races on the Continent. Scotland got its fair share of these and on one occasion, Nat Muir and I were the two

Scottish representatives at the big annual cross-country meeting in San Sebastian, Spain.

Our team manager was Ernie Devlin. He was an elderly gentleman and I believe he was Chairman or President of Scottish Athletics. For his selfless service to the sport he was rewarded with one overseas trip each year and this was it. We made a very bad impression on Ernie right the way through the weekend. He went out of his way to join us at every mealtime and was somewhat embarrassed as Nat and I complained about everything. We sent the meat back because it was undercooked and refused to drink the water provided.

History will show that Nat and I both ended up racing appallingly. It was disastrous. Ernie was required to file a debrief report back to Scottish Athletics when he returned from the trip. I heard some time later that it officially concluded: 'Muir and Williamson ran badly because they drank too much Fanta.'

✣ 54 ✣
CHRIS ROBISON

DURING my Royal Navy days, one of my running team-mates was coached by the legendary Gordon Pirie. We had a major track meeting in Plymouth but I had been troubled by a calf muscle strain for several weeks and decided not to race, hoping that a few more days of rest would still enable me to race in Gibraltar the following weekend.

Gordon was in Plymouth to watch one of his athletes and asked why I was spectating. I explained about the recurrent problems that I was experiencing with my calf and that I was trying to nurse it along for the following week. He said he swore by deep muscle massage for soft-tissue injuries and went as far as to offer some deep friction on my leg.

I was not aware of Gordon having any physiotherapy credentials but he insisted it had a good chance of success and marched me off to the changing rooms there and then.

'Lie down there' he said, pointing to a bench. 'You can swear at me as much as you like and get something to bite on. This will smart a bit but it will only last a minute.' Having identified the sore area on my calf, he then proceeded to grind his elbow into it hard for a minute. I have never known pain like it. I was screaming with agony. The tears were running down my face and at the end of the longest sixty seconds of my life, when I tried to stand on the leg, it gave way under me. Gordon was not finished yet.

As he propped me up he said 'Right you've got sixty seconds recovery and then we're going to go again.'

Escape was futile. I wasn't going anywhere on that leg. He assured me that it would not feel as painful second time around because it would be somewhat numb. After a further minute of agony my treatment was complete.

'If you stay off that for two more days and then jog for three days you'll be fine for next weekend.' Gordon assured me.

I doubted that very much but thanked him as I dragged my leg back to the stand with me. The most extraordinary aspect of all was that by the following weekend my calf was completely cured and I broke the course record for the Rock Race in Gibraltar!

✤ 55 ✤
GEOFF WIGHTMAN

THE last race which I ran in Southern California pretty much summed up my impressions overall of the local racing scene during my time as a student in that part of the world. It was the Del Mar 10k, a strange event, which was delayed 25 minutes on the start line because of the imminent arrival of a freight train at a level crossing.

There were around 800 runners and when we finally got under way, I was keen to make a good impression, having not raced for several weeks.

Approaching halfway I had built up a reasonable lead. Then came the bit that I had read about on the briefing notes but still found hard to believe. We dropped on to Del Mar Beach and had to run to the turnaround point, which was a flag-waving marshal. Unfortunately, as well as a misunderstanding on railroad timetables, the organisers had also had a bit of a problem with the high tide times.

The marshal was as close as he could get to the racing line but was up to his thighs in the sea. We had to go round him and then head back the way we came in, so I splashed back past 800 fellow runners, all of them weaving in and out of the surf, all of them cursing the course designer.

I managed to hold on to my lead and recorded 31.20. There was a very long wait until the prize-giving and the organisers decided to provide some entertainment for the people that had stayed on. One feature of this was a pancake-eating contest. Two members of the audience were selected at random. Their hands were tied behind their backs and a stack of pancakes were placed on a plate on the floor in front of each of them.

Using just their mouths, they had to race each other with the first to clear their plate being declared the winner. It was a faintly disgusting spectacle but everyone roared them on.

The winner was presented with his prize. It was a week for two, all expenses paid, skiing in Lake Tahoe. What? A $2,000 prize just for winning a random pancake-eating contest? Just imagine how lavishly they would reward the actual race winner if this was how they treated the sideshow.

It was with trembling hands that I gratefully accepted the winner's envelope from the race organiser. This man had gone up in my estimation. Never mind the level crossing and the high tide, he was clearly generous in his awards and I forgave him. I waited a discreet interval until I opened the envelope:

"Congratulations! You have won a complimentary one night stay at the Del Mar Hilton, currently under construction. It opens next October."

✤ 56 ✤
SUE RICHARDSON

FOR most of its first ten years, the London Marathon finish area was on Westminster Bridge. On one occasion I arrived early at the announcer's cabin on the Bridge to get ready for an eight-hour stint. Across the way, we watched as a crane lifted some portable toilet cabins high into the air from their position in a car park and set them down on the Embankment. As the last one was lowered into position, the door swung open and a man stepped out. The earth certainly moved for him that day!

✤ 57 ✤
GEOFF WIGHTMAN

WHEN I ran in the Barbados 10k in 1987, it rained very heavily an hour before the race. With a 3pm Saturday afternoon start, and the sun returning to raise the temperature into the 90s, the rain had upped the humidity to a greenhouse-like 90%. The race still started at a good pace and Gary Staines, who had broken through in a big way that summer, opened up a good lead.

By halfway he was about a hundred metres up on me and a lanky Dutch runner called Hans Koelman. This stayed the same beyond five miles and we talked about running in together. It suited me because the heat was getting really oppressive and I did not fancy a sprint finish. The rain had wiped out all of the chalk mile markers on the road but we agreed that there was less than a mile to go. The course kept twisting and turning and I kept thinking that each turn would be the last.

At that point I think I began to suffer heat exhaustion. It's a more sinister sensation than dehydration because it affects the senses more quickly, takes longer to dissipate and is potentially more serious. The crowds had grown bigger and I could not believe that we had still not entered the finishing straight. I felt dizzy and disoriented. Then, as we rounded yet another turn, I was quite convinced we were at the finish.

'There it is' I said to Hans and I veered to the right hand side of the road towards a small cluster of spectators.

'No, not there. Keep going,' Hans shouted.

I was hallucinating and the knot of spectators was not the finish. In fact they were just a group of innocent bystanders and they were a bit taken a back to see me plunge into their midst.

'Keep goin' man' I was urged.

'No, this is the finish', I gasped, as I lay sprawled on the floor.

'No man, the finish is round the corner'. That's what I had believed for the past five minutes. The thing was, the finish really was just around the corner. I was beyond the six-mile point but still had around 300 metres to go. For a while that didn't register with me as at all as I lay there, not able to remember who I was, let alone where I was.

The Race Director had received word that his equal second placer had veered off the course with less than a quarter of a mile to go and was last seen heading for the sea. He immediately set off for the beach in case I was intent on performing some weird Reggie Perrin kamikaze run into the surf.

After a while I came round and could tell from the stream of runners passing me that this was indeed not the finish line. I got back to my feet and tried to run again.

It was evident that my brain was still well and truly addled because I set off in the opposite direction, away from the finish line and back towards the incoming runners. A couple of my Dartford Harriers colleagues, who were out there on a racing holiday, passed me but they assumed I had already finished and was on my way to do a warm down jog, so they just waved to me.

Eventually the delirium cleared a bit and I turned round and started running in the same direction as everyone else. I finally made it across the finish line. The final 300 metres had taken me 11 minutes and I had lost 133 places.

✤ 58 ✤
GEOFF WIGHTMAN

THE only time I ever trained with the great Steve Ovett was at a Harry Wilson track session at Crawley one summer in the late 80s. Steve was going through a bad patch, having recently been beaten in the Southern 800m final and Harry had decided that a few sessions to re-tune his change of pace were in order. The training was to be something like 8-10 repetitions of 600 metres with the second half of each rep to be much quicker than the first. So, we would run each effort in about 90 seconds but it would be 50 seconds or slower for the first half and 40 seconds or better for the second half. The recovery jogs were, as I recall, hideously short.

The only other person taking part was Julian Spooner, someone I had known since schooldays in Kent. He dipped in and out of the session, probably doing around six of the reps. As a matter of pride, and because Ovett had been a hero of mine, I wanted to try and do the whole lot. It was clear from quite early on that Steve's fitness was coming back very quickly. I would generally lead through the first half and then he would power away in classic style over the closing stages.

I could not afford to be more than 3-4 seconds down because that would eat into the precious recovery time of less than a minute before we went again.

It was a very hard workout for me but Ovett was pushing himself as well. There was not much time for words to be exchanged because the cycle of surge-recover-surge was relentless. As we matched strides at the start of each rep and gasped in unison as we tried to recover at a jog between each effort I felt it was a bonding experience. We were both giving it all we had and there was a shared sense of suffering and common purpose. We would both be fitter athletes at the end of it and had helped each other through it.

At the end of the last interval we both staggered to the rail at the side of the track and hung our heads over the side, deep into oxygen debt. This was a training session to remember. Ovett was the first to recover his composure. He stood up and proffered a handshake to me.

'Thanks, Phil' he said.

✤ 59 ✤

NIGEL WALSH

FOR those of us who hail from South Africa, the annual Comrades Marathon, held over a 56-mile course between Pietermaritzburg and Durban each June, is a rite of passage. The course is hilly, an absolute brute, while the weather, although it's mid-winter, is often hot. Until recently, the finish cut-off was 11 hours. An 11:01 finish means no medal. At the cut-off, race officials turn their backs on the approaching runners and shut the finish funnel – all part of the race's charm.

On the third occasion that I ran the Comrades, I have my wife Colleen, who was then my girlfriend, to thank for my medal. She had driven to the 40-mile mark near Cato Ridge to cheer me on. Unbeknown to her I was having a real swine of a day. Long before halfway I had developed the mother of all blisters on one foot and was in agony at every footstrike. Limping heavily and feeling very sorry for myself, I was consoled by the knowledge I had only to get to 40 miles where I would be able to step off the road with dignity and be driven back home to Durban in comfort. If nothing else, that thought kept me going.

As I approached the throngs of spectators at Cato Ridge I spotted the familiar little white Volkswagen just beyond the village. I limped off the road, plonked myself down in her deckchair and announced: "I've had it, we're going home."

My better half was not in a sunny mood, being more than a little miffed at being kept waiting so long beyond my predicted arrival time.

Before I could say Polly Shorts she'd whipped off my shoes and socks. "What's wrong with my foot?" I whined. "You don't want to know," was the terse reply.

In seconds my feet were encased in fresh socks and my favourite old shoes and I was being hauled to my feet. "What do you think you're doing?" I asked as I was bundled unceremoniously back into the roadway. "I haven't sat out here all day in the sun just for you to announce you're bailing out ... get going, I'll see you at the finish."

With that she turned back to her car, jumped in, and roared off towards Pietermaritzburg, 16 miles away, in a cloud of dust.

I didn't know whether to laugh or cry. Another 16 miles on that wrecked, bleeding foot? I started hobbling ... I made it too, more than an hour before the officials turned their backs on the stragglers.

✦ 60 ✦
GEOFF WIGHTMAN

YOU might recall that John Campbell, New Zealand's answer to Alf Tupper, made an appearance in an earlier story with his off-beat approach to road relay running. We did not see that much of him in club events because he was cranking out international marathons on a regular basis, but he did stay true to form at the Rochester Road Relays, just before Christmas 1986.

Selecting the team's running order is always as headache but things looked like they were panning out pretty well for the mighty Dartford Harriers, with Andy Wilson challenging for the lead on leg 3. Campbell was preparing for leg 4. It is a rare thing indeed to see him standing still if he has running kit on so I am sure John would have been warming up from the moment the team convoy arrived at Rochester Airport, the venue for the race.

The course used for the relay threads its way through some administration buildings and then heads out and back to the farthest corner of the base. If you are spectating, there are no short-cuts to reach the turnaround point. It is just the same path out to the turnaround and back.

As Andy Wilson reached the turn, he was going well. He was, however, extremely surprised to find that the lone voice urging him on at this far outpost was none other than John Campbell. A brief conversation ensued from which our new member understood that he had to get back to the changeover at the same time, and by the same route as Andy Wilson, in full-on race mode.

Campbell, naturally, accepted this challenge and sprinted ahead of Andy all the way back to the changeover before heading out on leg 4. Just to add to the degree of difficulty, he performed his own dance of the seven veils as he went along, peeling off layers of clothing and even shedding the famous orange cagoule before setting off to run one of the fastest laps of the day.

✤ *61* ✤
ANGELA TOOBY-SMITH

THE Crystal Palace floodlit track meetings were packed to the rafters in the 1980s. It was always a brilliant atmosphere and British success helped to make them worthy of live prime-time TV coverage. At one such meeting, Steve Ovett's middle distance race was the grand finale and expectations were running high in what was a golden era for British mile running. The stadium was completely sold out.

An hour or so before his race, Steve went for a jog in the adjacent park area. As he returned, his entry to the Astroturf area was blocked by a steward.

'May I see your pass, please?'

Ovett hadn't taken his pass out on the warm-up with him and explained this to the steward. He also added that he was due to race the 1500 metres in less than thirty minutes time. This cut no ice at all with the steward – 'If you haven't got a pass you're not coming in.'

'My name's Steve Ovett and I'm running in the last race.'

'I don't care who you say you are, if you haven't got a pass you're not coming in.'

'Look I do need to get in here quickly to finish my warm-up, report in and get my spikes on.'

'If you haven't got a pass, you're not coming in.'

'There are plenty of people over there who will vouch for me.'

'If you haven't got a pass, you're not coming in.'

After some further remonstration and fraught pleading, it was agreed that the steward would ask for a call to be put out on the public address system for a meeting official to come to the gate and give a ruling. A few minutes later, someone duly appeared. 'For God's sake let him in, it's Steve Ovett' he cried as soon as he rounded the corner and saw the 1978 BBC Sports Personality of the Year being detained.

'Steve Ovett?' said the steward, as he finally opened the gate to let the anxious athlete sprint in 'Can I have your autograph for my kids?'

✣ 62 ✣

SUE RICHARDSON

I HAVE known Seb Coe since not long after he arrived on the international scene. On one occasion in the mid 80s, he was out training around Richmond Park when he noticed that one of the deer that roam free in the park was in some distress.

As a good citizen, he decided he should report this to the park rangers so knocked on the door of the small white lodge that is positioned by the Petersham Gate, just inside the park. It was true it did look very much like a park keeper's cottage. What Seb will not have realised is that, for three years of its existence, this unremarkable little building was the headquarters of the London Marathon organisation.

And that was where I worked, so you can imagine his surprise, when instead of a park warden, it was me who opened the door to our Olympic Champion, reporting a lame deer. I think he thought I must have been having a secret tryst with the park keeper!

✣ 63 ✣

GEOFF WIGHTMAN

ON my final weekend as a student at San Diego State University, I decided to venture into Mexico, with a team-mate, for a 10k road race. The event was just over the border in Tijuana and took place very early on a Sunday morning.

Despite this, it was extremely hot but with swirling winds whipping up a dust storm. There were about 500 runners for the 10k. All of the local heroes were in the line-up and the early pace was very quick. Within the opening two miles, a Mexican runner called Sosa had opened up a huge lead. I headed the chasing group and by the end I had managed to close the gap to less than ten seconds.

Our times were a shade over 30 minutes, which were not bad, given the conditions. At the prize-giving, I watched with astonishment as Sosa received a rapturous reception and was presented with a trophy the size of a bungalow. Then they gave him a television. Then they gave him a portable music centre.

This was indeed a surprisingly well endowed event and you can well imagine my sense of anticipation as I stepped up to be presented with the second place prize. It was just an envelope. Perhaps it was cash. When I stepped down, I discreetly opened it with my team-mate Juan and his family. To their credit, they didn't laugh as the fabulous prize was revealed. In the envelope was a voucher, redeemable at an establishment in Tijuana, which entitled the lucky winner to a free optician's appointment!

✧ *64* ✧
STEVE SMYTHE

IN the mid-80s I was staying at my parent's new home in Hornchurch, Essex. I needed to fit in a long run and, being unfamiliar with local routes, got out a map to work out the best loop to follow. It was baking hot, and as soon as I could, I moved off the roads on to some cooler wooded paths. Over time, this involved a few fences, stiles and farmyards but I pride myself on my sense of direction and was pleased when I rejoined the road for the later stages of my run. Rather more confusing was the dual carriageway that passed beneath the 'B' road that I was on. This had to be the A12 back towards Romford. I had been out for over two hours and was extremely tired and thirsty.

The A12, although somewhat uninspiring, was going to be my quickest route home so I scrambled down the bank and began running alongside the main carriageway. After about five minutes, a police car drew up and an officer asked what I was doing.

"Running to Hornchurch" I replied, although I would have thought it was a bit obvious.

'Not on the M25, you're not.'

It dawned on me that the map I had scrutinised did not have the newly built M25 on it and that actually I was going in the opposite direction to Hornchurch. Momentarily, I thought about being rude so that they would arrest me and take me home but it was clear from his demeanour that he was not keen on admitting a sweaty, bare-chested fly-covered runner. He pointed up the bank. I went.

Unfortunately the rest of the run did not go as planned and it was more than four hours in total before I staggered back on to my parent's driveway.

I do find it's a nice conversation stopper, when travelling on the M25 in Essex, to remark 'I used to train along the hard shoulder over there until the police stopped me.'

1990s...

Well done, Sally Gunnell

Our Olympian star

The public adored you, we knew you'd go far

You'd have run one lap faster

We're sure that you could

If your lane hadn't been littered

With those bits of wood

✣ 65 ✣
NICK ROSE

IT was a very good day for me when I won the masters division of the New York Marathon in the mid 90s. The organisers were pretty pleased as well and asked me to stay on for the post-race presentation party that evening but I couldn't. I was booked on an 8pm return flight that evening.

The British newspaper contingent were a bit mystified. 'Can't you change your flight?' one of them asked 'What do you have to get back for Monday morning for?' I kept my reasons to myself at the time. I thought there might be rather too much press mileage in the story if I had let it be known that the following morning at 10am, sharp, as it were, I had a longstanding appointment ... for a vasectomy.

✣ 66 ✣
JOHN NUTTALL

AFTER a hard race in Limerick, I was not able to provide a urine sample for doping control purposes immediately after the race. This was not unusual and the officials handed me some soft drinks to encourage nature to take its course. I think I must have downed three or four bottles and still nothing was happening. Then, quite suddenly, I was ready. I stood there with the sample beaker poised and the doping control officer observing expectantly. At that particular moment I could have peed for Britain as a litre or so of orange juice, water and Coke made itself available for immediate recycling. In a few seconds the sample beaker was full.

'Stop' said the doping control officer.

Stop? Have you ever tried stopping when you're mid-flow? It's virtually impossible. King Canute doesn't even come close. The beaker overflowed spectacularly. There were no other beakers handy and I had to continue with my personal Niagara Falls situation into the nearest suitable receptacle for the remainder of a minute and a half. A new PB.

✦ 67 ✦
MATTHEW YATES

I HAVE a vivid recollection of the Grand Prix meeting at Crystal Palace in July 1990. It was a beautiful summer evening, I was in good form in my first year at international level and the stadium was full. In my event, the 1500 metres, there was bound to be a lot of attention because it would be the last ever appearance on British soil by John Walker of New Zealand. He got a good reception when introduced and it seemed we were all set for another great night of middle distance running at this classic venue. The race was run at a good pace and there was a bit of a buzz in the crowd. As we entered the final lap, just ahead of us on the javelin runway, Steve Backley launched his latest effort.

My recollection is that as we got halfway down the back straight his javelin was still flying and it crossed my mind that he must have really got hold of it. In the shape he was in, that would probably prove to be the winning throw even against a world-class field. As we approached the 200-metre point, I decided to launch my bid for glory and moved into the lead. A tremendous roar went up. The atmosphere at Crystal Palace, at capacity, with 16,000 spectators can be electric but this was louder than anything I had heard since Ovett's heyday. It made the hairs on the back of my neck stand up. I was bringing the glory days back to Crystal Palace and the crowd was with me. Neil Horsfield of Great Britain was also with me and we entered the home straight neck-and-neck with the crowd still bellowing.

We both dived for the line and after scrutiny of the photo-finish he was given the verdict by 2/100ths of a second, with both of us recording 3:35. Unfortunately it did not take us long after crossing the line to spot the press photographers scuttling across to the javelin. Our cliffhanger race had actually gone completely unnoticed by the crowd and the media. Backley had just thrown a new world record, the first in Britain by a man since Dave Bedford in 1973. That was what all the noise was for. We were just a distraction.

♣ 68 ♣

GEOFF WIGHTMAN

WE used to live in the village of Ruddington, on the outskirts of Nottingham. One summer's evening I was just finishing a training run when I passed the village green. Up ahead, on a bench just back from the edge of the grass, I could see a large man, lounging back. It looked as if he might even have dozed off. From the distance, I could see that he had a dog lead wrapped around his hand. It couldn't have been much of a dog because the grass was a few inches overgrown and there was no sign of the dog at ground level. As he saw me approaching, he looked across and immediately tightened his grip on the lead. At the same time, the grass began to rustle and his dog started coming towards me, extremely rapidly through the grass. I was not too bothered. I don't like dogs but I had worked out which were the good and bad ones in our village and this one was tethered so I stayed on the racing line.

As it got to the edge of the pavement and emerged from the grass, the leash reached full tension and its momentum brought the animal up into the air on its back legs, where it hung, a couple of feet away from my legs, teeth bared, claws out and snarling. I jumped into the road. I couldn't help it. The man's pet that was having a go at me was actually ... a ferret.

♣ 69 ♣

LIZ BIRCHALL

BEFORE getting married, there was about a year when my husband to be, Rob (Birchall) and I lived apart before he was able to finish work and sell his flat in Birmingham. During this time I would regularly commute between Peterborough where I worked as publisher of *Athletics Weekly* and *British Runner*, and Birmingham.

It was a killer routine, which involved me tackling the M6 at the worst time on a Friday night on the way there, and a horrendous 5.30am alarm call so that I was on the road back to Cambridgeshire by 6am every Monday morning. Usually I would arrive at work on Monday mornings extra grumpy, slightly depressed and longing for Friday night to come around again.

One Monday upon arriving I sent him a slushy email to welcome him to work when he arrived. I am quite happy to gloss over the details of the content but suffice to say it opened with the phrase "morning my sweetie", and gradually degenerated into ever more slushy declarations of missing him and all the lovey-dovey stuff you could imagine ... I mean come on, we've all done it girls, right?

Unfortunately, as someone who receives a lot of athletics-driven emails mailed out to multiple addresses, I have my email system set to capture these addresses, and very often end up with an address book full of emails from people I've not even met.

I'm not quite sure how it happened, but for some reason – possibly the dozey Monday morning atmosphere had something to do with it – the email did not wing it's way to my fella but to another distance runner who I have never met in my life.

Credit the man for being so nice, I soon received a very polite email along the lines of 'Do I know you? If not thank you for your declaration of love, are you a poet, if not then you should be ... but I somehow believe I received it by mistake.' I was absolutely mortified, not only had I sent the email to the wrong person totally, but that it should be a Commonwealth Games representative and AAA champion.

Jon Wild, if you are reading this, once again, I'm sorry.

♣ 70 ♣
PAUL O'CALLAGHAN

I ONCE ran in a road race in Paris on a Saturday but had organised my racing commitments such that I needed to fly back for an event in Britain the following day. The schedule for return flights was extremely tight but the organiser had very kindly arranged for a taxi to be waiting for me just beyond the finish line to take me to Charles de Gaulle Airport. The race went well and I took fifth place. Because I ran a personal best time I had the luxury of a couple of minutes to warm down before jumping in the taxi. The taxi driver turned round to look at me, smiled and wished me 'bon arrivee' in his thick Gaelic tones. I smiled back. 'Early?' he said. 'Yes,' I replied, 'slightly early, so don't worry, we have plenty of time.' I was so tired that I dozed off for the whole 30 minute ride to the Airport. I was awoken as the driver pulled in to the drop-off zone. He turned round to wake me – 'Early!' he said. I looked out of the window. This wasn't my airport. 'Welcome to Orly Airport' said the large sign. That's what he'd been saying to me, not 'Early?' but 'Orly?'

Once we had cleared up the misunderstanding, our man drove like Schumacher across the city to Charles de Gaulle Airport. Far from dozing off, I was swinging from the safety strap on this leg of our tour.

Luck of the Irish – I was 90 minutes late but my flight had been delayed for three hours.

✢ *71* ✢
PETER HIER

ONE of the most spectacular venues used for the IAAF Cross-Country series was in Belfast, when they held the race in the grounds of Stormont Castle, which became the home of the Northern Ireland Assembly. It was very grand, with the huge main building hosting accommodation, restaurant and reception facilities. The first year it was staged there I remember making my way across the main lobby to head out into the grounds for the races. The entrance/exit was one of those revolving doors with three compartments, to prevent draughts getting into the building.

There was a man in the compartment just going out so I moved into the one behind. He appeared to be in some difficulty pushing the handle, so I leant against mine to keep the doors revolving.

Unfortunately the reason he was moving so slowly was because he was on crutches with his foot in a plaster cast, although I hadn't spotted this at the time.

This meant that my extra helpful push on the door handle sent my compartment pressing against his back and unfortunately overbalanced him so that just as his compartment came out into the air he stumbled forward and went sprawling all over the concrete slabs. I was mortified and rushed forward to help him to his feet. It was an accident but I thought this fellow might be angry at being knocked to the ground in his incapacitated state.

He seemed to take it quite well but you might imagine my further discomfort when I realised that the man that I had just pole-axed was none other than Sinn Fein leader, Martin McGuinness.

♣ 72 ♣
GEOFF WIGHTMAN

THE Commonwealth Games lived up to their reputation as 'The Friendly Games' in my experience because that was where I met my wife Susan (nee Tooby) in Auckland in 1990. The holding camp was in early January in Sydney and we used to go for late evening walks around the beautiful lakeside campus at Narrabeen.

One night, as I returned to my chalet from one of our little walks, at around 11pm, I was surprised to find that the lights were all out. My room-mates were all clean-living individuals – Jonathan Edwards, Chris Maddocks, Vernon Samuels and John King – but I felt a bit of a dirty stop-out.

I crept around in the dark, banging my knees against inanimate objects, and tiptoed off to the bathroom and back. About a minute after I had finally slid into my bed, by pre-arranged signal, all four of them started making snogging and slurping noises. They then proceeded to laugh their heads off, before springing back out of bed, fully-clothed, and turning the lights back on.

The blighters had posted a lookout for my return. Only one member of that chalet picked up a medal in Auckland – a somewhat surprise silver in the triple jump but twelve years later, for a few days in August 2002, he held a Grand Slam of Olympic, World, European and Commonwealth titles. Well done, Jonny Boy!

✣ 73 ✣

GARY LOUGH

I WAS quite nervous when I was warming up for the middle distance race at the Durham Cross-Country meeting a few years back. Our race would immediately follow the men's long race over five miles and that was being led handsomely by Britain's Jon Brown.

With a little under 15 minutes to our race start, I took myself off to a quiet corner of the field for some stretching and strides. Having stretched, I unzipped my shoe bag to put on my spikes. I was horrified to discover that I had packed two left shoes. With less than ten minutes to go, this was a cause for panic. I had no other racing shoes with me and I frantically began thinking about where I could get hold of some very quickly.

There was only one person at Durham who I knew for sure had spikes in my size with him. He was a former college team-mate of mine. Jon Brown.

As we have already noted, Jon Brown was otherwise occupied at this particular time in contesting the televised long race, and so, for that matter, were his spikes. He was well into the final lap. There was nothing for it. I would have to wait for him to cross the line and then borrow his spikes. I positioned myself alongside the finish chute and awaited his arrival. In the meantime the middle distance race was already reporting in, with just a couple of minutes to the gun.

Jon crossed the line to tremendous applause. I would have to get in quickly otherwise he would be in demand for press interviews.

"Jon," I called out "Can I borrow your spikes, please?"

He gazed across, blankly. It had been a very hard race.

I moved in alongside him.

"Can I borrow your spikes, please mate? I've brought two left ones."

He looked at me as if I was from the Planet Zarg. My predicament was not registering with him at all. I didn't have enough time left for him to recover his marbles. There was nothing else for it and I hastily began unlacing his spikes. This was by no means straightforward since they were caked in mud and my hands had become a collection of thumbs as the seconds ticked down.

I think by this stage Jon had grasped a little of what was going on and he stood patiently as I robbed him of his shoes and sped across to my race start, casting off clothing as I went. I did not look back but have this image of him then shuffling and sliding out of the finish area to meet the press, barefoot in the mud. At least he spared me having to do the same thing at speed.

Thanks Jon.

❖ *74* ❖
DUNCAN GASKELL

OVER the years, I have done less running training and substituted more cycling work. This is as a result of various lower leg injuries but can be quite galling because our company, K.I.M., has managed a huge number of elite athletes over the years and the opportunities for running, albeit very fast, have always been available.

There are some opportunities for off-road cycling in the parks around Teddington, where the company is based but my favourite is mountain bike work around the many routes near my former home, outside Halifax. There are a few canals in the area and the towpaths also enabled me to cross quite urban areas without ever seeing a car.

I must have cycled down the grassy bank onto one particular section of towpath hundreds of times but there is always that one time when things go pear-shaped.

As I applied the brakes, the bike started to slide from under me and I was propelled rather elegantly across the towpath towards the water with bike still attached to my feet courtesy of toe clips. It was as if in slow motion ... just as we are told these mishaps can appear to the unfortunate victim.

Surely I would not reach the water? It was too far away. Surely I would slow down? No. I went in, head first, my helmet hitting the canal bottom to arrest my descent.

But where was my bike? Fishing around in the chest-high water I located my weed-strewn mountain bike, which had been catapulted into the middle of the canal as part of the entry somersault.

I began to wonder how I would extricate myself from this black smelly location. A speedy exit with intact dignity was impossible as the sidewall was too high. I couldn't get a hand on top or anywhere near.

Unfortunately for my dignity, though fortunately for my health, workmen had been working nearby on a grassy bank.

"I wish I'd had a camcorder," said one of them. "That was brilliant!"

My voyeurs pulled me out and on I continued, now sodden, heavier than before and with 15 miles still to cycle home on that December day.

✤ 75 ✤
GEOFF WIGHTMAN

THE former BAF Road Running Commission used to meet on the eve of the Great North Run and one year the venue for the meeting was one of the hotels alongside the Metro Centre. After the meeting, most people stayed on for the race the next day and in the late afternoon I found myself in the adjacent McDonalds establishment dining on their finest haute cuisine with the national event coach for the Marathon, Gordon Surtees.

Gordon has had a long and distinguished career as a coach and, since this was 1997 I had almost, but not quite, forgiven him for not naming me as first reserve for the Barcelona Olympic team five years previously. We spoke about how many people were in Newcastle for the race and how our hotel was full to capacity.

'What type of room have you got?' asked Gordon.

This was an unexpected sort of question. 'Well it's the usual – bed, en-suite bathroom, desk, window overlooking the car park. Why?'

'Come and have a look at mine.'

So we trooped back to the hotel and headed for the top floor.

'This was the only room left' he explained as the lift opened onto the 'themed' floor.

'It's not exactly my cup of tea.'

He opened the door sheepishly. Inside, I was welcomed to the Wild West cowboy room. The walls were decorated with rawhide leather. The en-suite bathroom was the 'County Jail', the bedside chair was a bucking bronco from which Gordon could watch the television and I fell about laughing when I saw where he would be sleeping – a full size chuck wagon, complete with hooped canopy, raised four feet off the ground.

I am sure he slept soundly that night, safe from Red Indian ambush twelve floors above the Gateshead Metro Centre.

♣ *76* ♣
SAM LAMBOURNE

SEVERAL years ago I was working in the Jog Shop when 'Dynamic Dave' a trade rep and photographer came in, as he often did. He showed me a pair of shoes that the Asics promotions manager had given him in exchange for taking some photos.

They must either have been pretty bad photos or something had gone amiss because they were the somewhat ancient Asics 120 model in size 8 and green. Unfortunately they were also two left shoes.

I had no real use for them but thought maybe I could cut them in half as a demonstration pair, or something, so I accepted them with gratitude, put them in the back of the stockroom and promptly forgot all about them.

It was only a few months later that a customer from Eastbourne came in to the shop. He was disappointed that, having discovered a training shoe that he had trained in exclusively for three years, he was finding it very difficult to track down replacement pairs.

He liked them so much that he had gone out and bought the last pair he could find anywhere in the UK. Unfortunately his dog had immediately elected to eat one of this prized pair, leaving him with a souvenir brand new right shoe and a left shoe that was shredded and in pieces.

He had brought just the one right shoe into the shop with him, in the forlorn hope that I could find a solution to his problem. I took a look at the shoe. I was amazed to see that it was an early model Asics 120 in green and it was size 8.

'Hang on there a minute' I said 'I'll just have a look in our 'three years old left shoe department' to see if I have an Asics 120 in green, size 8.'

I promptly brought out one of Dave's shoes from the stockroom. I didn't charge the bloke anything for this and I really don't think he thought there was anything unusual in what I had done.

I rushed out that evening after work and bought a ticket for the lottery, utterly convinced that I just couldn't fail to win. Unfortunately I must have used up all of my astronomical odds lucky shots for that day, and probably a few more days as well.

✣ *77* ✣
GEOFF WIGHTMAN

THE European Athletics Championships were held in Split, then part of Yugoslavia, in the summer of 1990. The men's marathon was held on the final day of competition, with a brutal 4pm start on a four-lap course that offered precious little shade.

The temperature was still up in the 80s when the field of around 70 runners headed out of the stadium towards Split harbour front. Having been held on the start line for ten minutes or so, most runners were planning to make good use of the first drinks station at the 5k mark. Alas, this was to be the point where one of our happy band bade farewell to the race.

The problem was that some distance before the drinks area, the organisers had thoughtfully positioned a sponge station. This came upon us unexpectedly, just as the members of the tightly packed field were steadying themselves, in readiness for the drinks pick-up. In the group around me, things happened very fast. The first runner made a lunge for the sponges, which were in tubs on the table, missed completely and caught the tub with his hand. The table, which was only one of those round white plastic garden furniture items, began to rock backwards and forwards, causing the second runner to missed the target as well.

His hand also thumped the table and it fell sideways, spilling the bowls and sponges all over the place. The really bad news for runner number three was that the table had a large parasol which fell right into his path.

By some extraordinary feat of gymnastics, in attempting to get out of the way, he succeeded only in getting one leg either side of the parasol stem. In this ungainly straddling manner, he was unable to stop himself from plunging right into the canopy of the parasol. He let out a loud curse as he went down.

I think he was Bulgarian.

My last sighting off him was as his fall triggered the release mechanism and the canopy began to close round him like some sort of giant Venus fly-trap.

What a cruel end to months of preparation, less than three miles into a major Marathon. It's one thing hitting the wall but imagine having to return to family and friends and explain that you were eaten by an umbrella.

✣ 78 ✣

BILLY BURNS

BEFORE I made it as a marathon runner and qualified for the Commonwealth Games in 1998, my background was as a mountain runner. I was not aware of being particularly hardy but one episode made it clear that your discomfort threshold does go up a few notches when you're running on the hills regularly.

I travelled on my own for a training spell on Mount Teide in Tenerife. I rode there by mountain bike and wheeled it the rest of the way up to the summit and pitched my tent ready for some good training the next day. I was conscious that the weather was closing in a bit as I made my way up. It seemed to be nothing out of the ordinary, although the wind was whistling a bit as I settled into my tent for the night. Unbeknown to me the weather was a cause for a full-scale emergency and with blizzards through the night, the mountain was evacuated. The storm lasted for three days, and I only left the tent every two hours to clear the snow off the roof to stop it collapsing. I survived on energy bars for this period.

At the end of this storm I left the tent ready for some training to find the snow had drifted much more than I expected and it was clearly going to be too deep for running. I packed up my tent and began heading back.

Much further down the mountain my appearance caused quite a commotion. There were emergency and rescue personnel and vehicles all over the place. They were on the lookout for any overnight victims being in a bad way. I did not quite fit the bill as a casualty of the storm, strolling down, wheeling my bike. One TV news crew stopped me to ask how on earth I had survived the worst snow blizzards for years. They asked if I would mind lying down on a stretcher to put the weather into context, so I lay down and was shown on lunchtime news being lifted into a waiting ambulance. Someone held on to my bike while this was filmed and then I was on my way again.

❖ 79 ❖
CHARLIE MUSSETT

THE wife of one of our Great North Run organising team had a most unfortunate episode in the race two years ago. Approaching halfway she was bursting for a wee and could not wait for the next set of portable toilets. Just up ahead was some undergrowth up against the fence of the dual carriageway so she veered off the road and sped through the bushes right to the fence. After a moment of blissful relief she had just re-arranged her clothing and was just about to get up from her crouching position when a fellow competitor came bursting through the bushes.

In his desperation he had not seen her and before he could have got sight of her he began backing towards the fence with his shorts dropped round his ankles, mooning for Britain, and clearly intent on an urgent number two. What was our lady to do? He was still backing towards her. Where would it all end? She made a genteel cough – 'Ahem'.

The man looked round, mortified. 'Oh my God!' he squawked, pulling up his shorts and sprinting out of the bushes He disappeared back into the race in two seconds flat, forgetting all about the motion that he had set in motion, as it were.

❖ 80 ❖
GEOFF WIGHTMAN

ONE of the biggest schools in Bristol is in Mangotsfield and my wife Susan had one of her first teaching posts there. For three months after we got married, we lived in nearby Olveston and were invited to help 'hare' the area schools cross-country championships at Mangotsfield.

There were three boy's races and three girl's races. The course was on two levels. The upper level was playing fields and followed a simple perimeter loop. Down the bank was a more intricate area of heather and wooded paths. It was also marked by flags and pupils acting as marshals. After the five youngest races, my fellow hares had had enough and the Senior Boys were to be my sole responsibility.

All went well for the first circuit. I ran about forty yards ahead of a lead group of five or six boys. By the time we dropped down onto the wooded paths, there was one breakaway runner. As we reached the furthest point on the course, he had a lead of about twenty yards. At that point there was a hairpin turn on the course.

It was a fairly obvious turn because directly ahead there were houses being built, just the other side of a bridge. Unfortunately, the marshal who had earlier been manning this post had decided he had finished for the day and as we drew near there was nothing to indicate the turn. I slowed right down so that the leader could see me and extravagantly indicated a left with my arm. It was thick foliage but, as I doubled back, I could see him approach.

I was ten yards past the turn. He was ten yards before the turn. He looked across. 'Next left round to here' I shouted and then set off to re-establish the gap which haring protocol requires. The path then twisted and turned so I could not get a sighting back to him. It was more than 30 seconds before I got a look back.

There was no sign. The stupid basket had gone straight on! There was a field of almost 200 runners following him. By the time I could get back to the turn, probably over a third of the field had headed out towards the building site, presumably including a certain number of Mangotsfield runners who were on home territory.

What do you do in that situation? I shouted down the trail and ran after some of the runners streaming ahead but they ignored me. I then went back to the corner and led the next group of runners round the turn and then directed them all the way back to the finish. Over the next thirty minutes or more the scenes on those playing fields were not pretty. It was like something from the Battle of the Somme. Boys arrived from every direction you could think of.

Some were covered in building sand, some had run straight into brambles, others had had to scale fences to get back. Many were in tears. Teachers were shouting. Some of the parents started arguing and pushing each other. It was desperate. It was a long time before they could even do a head count. The race was declared void amidst angry recriminations and re-staged three weeks later on a date when I was 'unavailable'.

✤ *81* ✤
JACKIE NEWTON

I HAVE run the Manchester Marathon on numerous occasions. I'm from Stockport so it is my local marathon and I love it. I have been lucky enough to win it on one occasion so it was a real low point when I had to drop out before the halfway point six years ago.

With my local knowledge, I knew that the best way of getting back to the finish area to pick up my kit and meet my family was going to be to get on a train so, just a few minutes later, I was sitting on a crowded local train, feeling very sorry for myself, when the ticket inspector walked in.

'Tickets, please' he announced to a full carriage.

When he got to me, I explained my situation and that I had neither a ticket nor money on me. My story will have sounded quite plausible, given that I was sitting there still moderately sweaty in a crop top and running briefs and wearing a race number. Nobody else was dressed like that and it would have been a relatively elaborate ruse for a fare-dodger to pull, especially the sweaty bit.

The man appeared unmoved.

'I am sorry' he said extremely loudly ' I am going to have to charge you a penalty fare'

I protested that I had no means of paying the fare.

'I am afraid that is no excuse' he bellowed even more loudly. 'I am going to have to issue you with a penalty notice.' He took out his notebook and pen.

'What is your name and address?' he shouted.

A bad day was getting worse. Wearily, I gave my details. He flourished his pen and then, quite suddenly lurched forward towards me. It was a bit alarming.

'Now' he whispered very quietly 'I am pretending to write out the penalty notice and hand it over to you so that the rest of the carriage will not think I have let you get away with it. If we're not careful, everyone will try it.' He stood up, winked and was on his way.

♣ 82 ♣
PETER ELLIOTT

THE city of Split in Croatia has had a dramatic few years but, when it was still part of Yugoslavia, it played host to the 1990 European Athletics Championships. Britain had an extraordinarily successful week, winning most of the men's track events, so on the final night, after a brief but lively dinner back at the team hotel, many of us headed into the centre of town.

We were hardly the Wild Bunch. The group included David Sharpe, Matt Yates, Neil Horsfield, Ian Hamer, Richard Nerurkar, Gary Staines and about four others whose identities I forget. One of our number started dancing with a couple of the local girls. This irritated one of the local boys who came over to object and began to cause a ruck. Before he could get too far with this, the bouncers intervened and, seeing that he was drunk, threw him out.

This did nothing for his frame of mind, and when we emerged as a group some while later, he and his pals were waiting for us. We sized up the situation very quickly and began running. We were good at running. After all that is what we were there for. In a relatively short distance the other Yugoslavs/Croatians had given up, apart from the original troublemaker and his mate, who kept galloping after us all the way down to Split Harbour, where our escape options became rather more limited.

It was at this point that we noted, with some disquiet, that he was wielding a hammer in a threatening manner, making lunges at us. It was time to disarm him. Several of the boys overpowered him and threw the hammer into the harbour. The man himself was still swinging, though, so we threw him into the harbour as well. He made a hell of a splash and re-surfaced screaming blue murder. It would have taken him some while to get out because the harbour walls were high but by that time most of us had made an extremely speedy and diplomatic retreat back to the Team Hotel.

The episode was not without some personal risk and the hero was David Sharpe who took a hammer blow to his arm. In the heats of the men's 1500m, I had been tripped but was re-instated for the final which I had ran earlier that evening with one arm strapped. It has always surprised me that when we left Split the following morning on a flight that was full of journalists and which was greeted by a battery of photographers at Heathrow, nobody enquired how it was that, the day after my race, David came to have his arm equally heavily bandaged as well.

❖ *83* ❖

RICHARD NERURKAR

I RAN the 10,000 metres at the Barcelona Olympics. It was a terrific Games and I enjoyed it all the more for the fact that a large group of family and friends had travelled to Spain to support me. Security is generally very tight in and around the athlete's village but during the second week it became very much more relaxed – so much so that the checks carried out on the accreditation passes for those entering the athlete's village got much slacker and it became very easy to bring guests into the village on team-mates' passes.

Keen to show many of my friends how great the facilities were inside the village, I was one of those who readily took advantage of this. After a number of successful entries by some of my friends, I was on the hunt for another willing team member from whom I could again borrow a pass to use for another of my friends. Before long someone stepped forward with her pass to allow me to invite my friend Lucy into the village.

Having had a walk round the village, just before she left, we decided to call in at one of the many village restaurants for an ice-cream. As we were entering the restaurant, one of the guards on duty noticed a misfit between Lucy's face and the photograph on the pass around her neck.

We were summarily arrested – yes, the village police, we now discovered, could be quite strict – and Lucy was escorted out of the village and her pass confiscated. Meanwhile I was called into one of the security offices to give an explanation for my actions. My biggest concern was knowing how to retrieve the confiscated pass – especially since the pass would be required to give (even officially accredited) athletes access to the village restaurants.

So my fellow team member who had helped me out had to go without meals for the rest of the day, or at least rely on her friends to bring food out of the restaurants for her, and wait until the pass was returned. In the end the GB Chef de Mission had to present himself personally at the Village Security Office to issue a formal apology, after which the pass was returned.

What made owning up to my crime in front of the British team management more embarrassing by the fact that Lucy is blonde and slight and less than five feet tall and the photo ID pass which she was wearing so nonchalantly belonged to Myrtle Augee, our very well-built black shot-putting star.

✣ 84 ✣
HUGH JONES

MY wife, Cheryl, is from Barbados and over the years, I have run the Barbados Marathon 13 times. I've won six times but this occasion was one of my two career DNFs. The race begins at the airport well before dawn but two and a half hours later as I neared the finish the heat and humidity were searing. I had built up a lead of several minutes over second place but with little more than a minute to run, I collapsed with heat exhaustion.

Anxious to finish the job, I tried to get to my feet but I had lost all sense of balance. I raised myself on all fours and tried to crawl but even that was too much. I lay there with my brain scrambled and my limbs powerless but with competitive instinct still intact.

By hook or by crook, I was determined to reach the finish line. There is an Indian fakir who once rolled for 2,000 miles to the site of a holy shrine. That was it. I would roll to the finish. There's more than one way to complete a marathon. I lay on my side and began rolling in the general direction of the finish line. It was not to be. I had made it down the road a few yards – about 2,000 miles less than the fakir – when the medics rushed the 250m back from the finish and carted me off to hospital. I was spared one embarrassment. The TV crew had already gone to the finish to film my triumphant arrival, but they were not so quick to respond to my condition as the medics. They decided to edit their footage so that both my long-time lead and my little mishap never appeared on the coverage.

✦ 85 ✦

NIGEL GOUGH, CHARLIE MUSSETT, DAVID HART

AT the Great North Run three years ago, we had a very good record on medical mishaps. The only person who was detained overnight in hospital was someone who had successfully completed the race but then had overdone the celebrations in the beer tent afterwards and had to be treated for their paralytic condition.

THE distinction for having completed the shortest distance in the Great North Run was achieved the previous year. With 30,000 and more competitors, the starting masses can stretch back for half a mile down the A1. It usually takes 10 or 15 minutes for the front ranks to clear and for the back markers to cross the start line proper. This was too much for one supremely conditioned athlete.

Having finally made it to the official start line, he pronounced himself 'completely knackered' and dropped out. He stepped off having covered just two metres of the race.

ONE year, one of the punters decided to travel by train to Newcastle, already dressed in the gorilla costume that he intended to wear for the race. Unfortunately for our gorilla, he left home way too late and, having run all the way to the start from Newcastle station, he discovered the race was already under way.

He dashed across the start line and threw his wallet to one of the marshals. 'Look after that for me, mate' he shouted as he sprinted into the distance. The marshal called after him but the gorilla was not stopping for anyone.

We have a chain of vehicles that can get emergency items or personnel from the Great North Run start line to the finish at South Shields. It is not intended to be used for gorilla's wallets but that was its purpose on this occasion.

So, a couple of hours later the wallet was handed to Max Coleby who was working on the finish line.

'We were handed this by a bloke dressed as a gorilla' he was told.

'Well how the hell am I supposed to get it back to him?' asked Max, looking down at the wallet and scratching his head. At that very moment it was snatched from him by a gorilla as he crossed the finish line.

'That's my wallet. Well done lads. Thanks for looking after it.'

✣ 86 ✣
BRUCE TULLOH

ON one occasion I was running around, spectating at a race in Sutton Park, Birmingham. Just after I had passed a couple of locals out walking their dog, the man said in a very loud Brummie accent: 'You never see an old jogger y'know. They're all dead by the time they're sixty.'

✣ 87 ✣
GEOFF WIGHTMAN

THE Commonwealth Games men's marathon had a 7am start down by the waterside in Auckland in January 1990. Ahead of the race there was much talk about the quality of the small field of 30 runners, including as it did, the top two men in the world through the 1980s, Rob de Castella and Juma Ikangaa. Also in the line-up were Steve Jones, Steve Brace and Steve Moneghetti. The outstanding favourite was Douglas Wakiihuri of Kenya, the reigning world champion and Olympic silver medallist from Seoul.

We were kept in a corralled grass area between the road and the waterside. There was a marquee and a few other amenities, including some portable toilets, dotted about. Most runners went for a short jog and then headed back to the enclosure to stretch and change shoes. With less than 15 minutes to the start, I headed for the portable loo furthest from the marquee. I joined a queue with just one other person. It was the Zen-like figure of Wakiihuri. We made no communication with each other, not even eye contact. Men don't engage each other when they are queuing for the traps.

For us, there is just one exception to this golden rule and Wakiihuri was about to invoke that exception. After two or three minutes of waiting patiently, he stepped forward and knocked on the door. We exchanged a 'what's he up to in there?' look. Another minute went by and he stepped up to the oche again, gave the door handle a sharp tug and shouted 'Hurry up'. Another minute went by and we did not have all that much time left to the start. It was all beginning to get a bit panicky and there was no alternative amenity in sight. We exchanged another old-fashioned look. Maybe there was a major incident in the making – 'Oh dear what can the matter be, Rob De Castella is locked in the lavatory.'

It was time for action. Douglas, my new queue buddy strode forward once again. He gave another 'Everything all right in there?' shout and, with no response, yanked at the handle. With that the door flew open, revealing an unoccupied throne. We had been waiting for five minutes outside an empty convenience. We both cracked up. A little over two hours later he won the Commonwealth marathon title with a devastating sprint finish.

I like to think I helped settle his nerves.

♣ 88 ♣
JOYCE SMITH

MY brother-in-law David decided to give running a go for the first time in his late 40s. He was pleasantly surprised to find that he took to it very quickly and was soon running every day. There was only one thing that troubled his new regime. He had a favourite loop that took him out and back across fields but at the beginning and end of the loop there was a back garden containing a fierce dog. Almost every time he passed, it would burst out of the garden and come nipping at his ankles. There was never any sign of an owner and nothing seemed to deter this dog. David was loathe to stop using the route but was growing heartily sick of its aggressiveness.

One time, as he neared the back garden at the start of the loop, he saw a large stick on the ground and picked it up, ready to take a swing at the dog if it came near. As luck would have it, for once, there was no sign of the dog.

As he passed the gap in the garden he breathed a sigh of relief, discarded the stick and headed out for a very pleasant run. He still had to negotiate Rover's lair on the return run. As he got close to the garden, he began peering intently to see if there was any likelihood of an ambush. In fact he was peering so intently that he did not see the large stick, which he himself had thrown away some minutes earlier. His foot landed awkwardly on top of the stick, spraining his ankle. It immediately swelled up like a balloon and he had to limp slowly all the way back home.

✣ *89* ✣
ANDY SMITH

DURING the twenty years that I have been racing, I have never once picked up a prize. It looked very likely that a North Yorkshire League race a few years back was going to change all that. Everyone knew that the top ten senior men's finishers got prizes. They always did. It was a generously deep set of awards.

Even my dear old mother who was spectating knew that. I ran surprisingly strongly in the second half of the race, probably the best run of my life, and with less than a mile to go I could see all of the leaders ahead of me. I was in 11th and closing rapidly on the man ahead. As we entered the finishing straight, I needed to time my sprint finish to catch him unawares and give him no opportunity to react. Trying to keep my breathing and footfall as quiet as possible, I moved out to one side. He was struggling and didn't seem to be aware that I had closed him right down. This was the moment. I was going to be gracing the awards ceremony with my presence for the first time ever. I would do it in style. I was ready to strike.

At that precise moment my mother decided to bellow some surprisingly loud encouragement from the sidelines, a few yards away.

'Go on Andy! You're in 11th. If you pass him you're in the top 10'.

This undoubtedly transformed the race for me in a marked manner. No sooner had mum kindly mentioned that 10th prize was up for grabs than a miraculous recovery took place in my previously demoralised opponent. He glanced over his shoulder and saw me alongside him. He also became belatedly aware that he was holding the last of the prizes and from nowhere at all became very motivated indeed about hanging on to that vital position.

He held me off by a second all the way to the line.

✣ 90 ✣
BASHIR HUSSAIN

I RAN in the Hong Kong Marathon one year. It's a long flight from the UK, so when I was offered a Chinese massage at the race HQ the night before the race, I jumped at the opportunity, believing it would remove any lingering stiffness before the next morning's race.

The masseuse really applied a lot of pressure. She went in very deep on my back muscles. It was one of those rubs where it was quite aggressive but I could feel it getting rid of the tightness so I was happy that she knew what she was doing. I was slightly less happy to find that at one point she was sat astride my back, in order to apply even more pressure on her thumbs. I thought that would be a difficult one to explain to my girlfriend if she walked in.

After about twenty minutes she was finished and I seemed noticeably looser and less tense as I walked away. The following morning I actually won the Hong Kong Marathon and felt quite comfortable in doing so. The local TV station interviewed me immediately after the race. The interviewer congratulated me on my win and said that it was all the more remarkable, given the heavy fall that I had suffered.

'I didn't fall over' I said.

'We thought you must have done because of the heavy bruising that was plain to see all across your shoulders and back.'

This concerned me and as soon as I could I got to a mirror in the changing rooms. I looked like I'd been set about with a baseball bat and then involved in a car crash. The whole of my back was a mass of angry welts and bruises. Her most outstanding work appeared to be the long symmetrical line of purple circles that stretched either side of my spine, starting at my neck. It looked terrible but the moral of the story is: Get a violent Chinese massage whenever you can before a big race! It was 1996. The bruises have gone now.

2000
and beyond

Paula's our new star – the world number one

And two million Brits are now running for fun

It's cheap and it's friendly and your heart gets

much stronger

And dear friends will purr that you keep it up longer

But how will you celebrate this age of the 'noughties'

In impeccable style – with more FUNNY RUNNING

SHORTIES!

❖ 91 ❖
PAUL LARKINS

A COUPLE of years ago I was invited to Hawaii to cover the Honolulu Marathon on behalf of *Running Fitness* magazine. I decided that I would actually have a run in the event and carry my Nikon camera with me to record the sights along the way. I was reasonably fit at the time and set off at around three-hour pace, even with my trusty Nikon.

The race starts very early in the morning because of the high temperatures that can be reached by mid morning. We had been running for about an hour and it was still well before sunrise. I began to experience mild stomach cramps and decided that I would take a pit stop at the next convenient opportunity.

Sure enough, within a mile, we passed by a line of portable loos and I headed for the nearest one. As the door closed behind me it was pitch black but one cubicle is very much like another in the world of portable toilets and I put my camera on the ledge alongside me and sat down to take care of business. Afterwards, it was still difficult to see anything so I opened the door slightly as I made ready to collect my camera and rejoin the Marathon.

The pre-dawn light revealed a most unfortunate state of affairs. One of the previous speedy competitors must have also made a hasty visit to this compartment – a little too hasty because he (or she) had missed the target by a long way and on the side ledge, some way from the aperture, was a very large, and still steaming, turd. Worse still, in the darkness, I had placed my beloved £250 Nikon camera about one millimetre away from it. It was a very cautious retrieval process.

❖ 92 ❖
MALCOLM CROFT

THE Trans 333 is a mad event, which I ran in December 2001. It is held in Niger, West Africa, and is a stage race that takes place over 333 kilometres of mostly desert running. There were only 90 starters and less than half completed the course. The extreme heat is the major factor with temperatures well above thirty degrees all day long. It is also quite easy to go off course.

The medical supervision is stringent. They detected someone hobbling very slightly with knee swelling in the early kilometres and withdrew him from the race. I covered the first 100k or so of race just inside the top twenty. I was going quite well until just beyond 100k when my running action started to go a bit uncoordinated.

One of the French medics called me over. He claimed I was suffering dehydration. I disputed this and got surprisingly aggressive in arguing the point. When I look back on it now I can see that I was completely out of it and was probably ranting like a madman at him. He insisted that I sit down in the shade and drink a bottle of isotonic fluid, which he would provide. I agreed to this, the understanding being that if I could drink it all, I could carry on.

He then produced a plastic container the size of one of those water dispensers that you see in offices. It must have contained twelve gallons. I went loopy again but he was insistent. Over the next couple of hours I drank as much as I could of this potion. The fluid soon worked its way through the system and I had to relieve myself a number of times. On each occasion I took great delight in peeing up the side of his Land Rover wheel. This did not improve relations much and in my addled state I hatched a cunning plan.

While he was engaged in speaking to other officials and competitors, I would sneak round the other side of the vehicles and re-join the race. Once his back was turned I set off, quite fast but, on reflection, weaving a bit of a mazy line. I had not got very far when the good doctor drew alongside in his Land Rover, with one wheel shinier than the rest.

'Where do you think you're going? He asked quietly.

'I'm rejoining the race and you can't stop me' I bellowed.

'I'm afraid I can' he replied. 'The race goes down that road back there behind us. You've just headed out in completely the opposite direction. It's desert for a hundreds of kilometres without any recognised trails the way you're going.'

I officially withdrew from the Trans 333 that evening but I'll be back.

✣ *93* ✣

TOM MAYO

IT'S always very reassuring when you arrive at an overseas destination for a race to be met by the hosts as soon as you clear the door from the airport customs hall. So, when I took part in the Stockholm Grand Prix meeting a couple of years ago, given that the organisers are renowned for their efficiency, it was no surprise that as soon as I came through the doors into the arrivals hall, the nearest person directly opposite me was a driver holding one of those little placards with 'MAYO' written neatly on it.

'Hi, I'm Tom Mayo' I introduced myself and we shook hands.

He welcomed me to Stockholm and I followed him out to the car. We made small talk as we threaded our way out of the airport complex and through the surrounding neighbourhoods.

We had been driving for about half an hour when I asked him where I would be staying.

'Well, on the boat I guess' he replied. We were heading towards the harbour at this point. What a nice touch by the organisers. We were going to be accommodated in a floating hotel on the waterfront. Very refreshing.

'And how far is that from the stadium?' I enquired.

'What stadium?'

'The athletics stadium where the track meeting is taking place.'

'What track meeting?'

We continued at cross-purposes for a short while longer before the awful truth dawned on us both. He had been waiting for a completely different 'Mayo' at the airport and I had just been driven twenty miles, probably in the wrong direction by a random stranger. We shot back to that airport arrivals lounge in double-quick time.

✤ 94 ✤
NICK TROOP

ON one occasion, I joined a group of our *Runner's World* readers for a coaching week in Davos, Switzerland. We were preparing to race a 30k event in the mountains the following weekend. I learned a little bit about mountain running over the course of that week but I also learned once again, that where runners are concerned, you can't judge a book by its cover. One morning we were out with the group, covering a regular 6k loop. It was early in the week and every one of us was having problems getting used to the effects of high altitude.

I hung back to keep an old boy company. He was clearly really struggling. He looked very laboured and he seemed to be having great difficulty breathing. Worst of all, he seemed to be limping heavily. It was a shame. He had come all that way but was clearly in no shape to race.

'How's it going?' I enquired.

'Not too bad' he just about managed to gasp back. It was almost certainly his first ever run at altitude so no wonder he had been knocked for six by the thin air, what with that and his injury.

'Going to try the 30k on Saturday?' I continued, mostly out of politeness. 'No', he replied. That was a relief. He'd never get round. After a brief pause he continued 'I'm doing the whole thing'

What? Surely some mistake here? 'The whole thing' was the full 78 kilometres of the Davos Mountain Marathon, including thousands of metres of ascent through the dreaded Sertig Pass. He would need an air ambulance. He must have been joking.

'Have you run here before?' I persevered.

'Oh, yes' he said 'I've done the race a couple of times before.'

It turned out that the old boy was Dave Phillips, not only one of the UK's most prolific ultra distance runners but also a founder member of the Marathon 100 Club – his 'couple of times' was actually 12 previous complete races.

His breathlessness was caused by the fact he had flown in late the night before and it was his first run that morning. In reality he probably ran more miles before breakfast than I did in a month. He duly finished the full Mountain Marathon with ease.

❖ 95 ❖
LISA HEYES

AS my running has improved hugely over the past couple of years, it has proved to be the right career move for me to switch from being an operating theatre assistant to becoming a community dietetic assistant (dietician).

I enjoyed the nursing work but emergency surgery sessions could be mentally and physically very draining. I thought I had learned how to cope with the day to day traumas but, when my husband Guy and I were first going out, it became evident that some of those experiences were staying with me.

I have always been prone to sleepwalking and in the early hours of one night when we were staying at his parent's house, apparently, Guy awoke to find me creeping into his room. I then spent the next few minutes slowly 'laying him out' in the manner of a recently deceased person. He lay there in silence, very alarmed, as I finished by folding his arms across his chest and closing his eyelids. Just to really freak him out, it would appear that, before returning to my room I said aloud 'Are you quite sure there is nothing more that can be done for him doctor?'

❖ 96 ❖
ANDY EDWARDS

PICTURE the scene: the first day of the European Indoor Athletics Championships 2002 in Vienna. Tim Hutchings and I are just packing our things away at the commentary point, having completed an eight hour, yes eight hour, stint on air for Eurosport Television. A technician from Austrian television comes round to our area as we are putting the stats and marker pens away.

He approaches me and asks for my autograph. This was well and truly a first. I asked him why he wanted it.

'You're a runner, aren't you?'

Now I did manage to break 3 hours at the inaugural London Marathon in 1981 but I thought it unlikely that I would be a hero in Austria 21 years later on the strength of that run. At this point it is also pertinent to mention that I am 48 and Caucasian.

'I do run but I'm not famous, you should ask one of the others.'

'But you're Derek Redmond'

'What?'

Then I noticed him looking at the accreditation pass hanging around my neck. It was true, it did say 'Derek Redmond' but that was only because Derek had been scheduled to partner Tim on his Eurosport debut, only to come down with food poisoning the day before departure.

I had been a late substitute and the accreditation was still in Derek's name. He still took a bit more persuading that no, I was not the man who set the British 400-metre record in 1987. He finally asked me, pointing at Tim: "Is that Tim Hutchings?" My reply was "I promise you, that is Tim Hutchings!"

✤ 97 ✤
GEOFF WIGHTMAN

MY idea of what constitutes a long traffic jam was completely revised when our family was stuck on the M1 in September 2002. We were travelling north to Nottingham for the Robin Hood Half Marathon the next day but had arranged to see friends for lunch on the Saturday. By 12.30 we were just south of Leicester and rang ahead to say that we would be arriving at about one o'clock.

A few minutes later we were stationary and the indicator boards suggested that the M1 had been closed.

We learned much later that this was the police response to an 'incident' where someone had to be talked down from a bridge across the motorway near the services.

Quite why this should have taken as long as it did is not clear but it was more than SEVEN hours before we reached the next exit and it was 8.30pm when we finally arrived at our hotel, just 20 miles north of the initial hold up.

There was only one thing that enlivened proceedings and that was a local radio station inviting people to send text messages to them on their early evening programme. We sent messages in a variety of pseudonyms and were very entertained when they were read out. However, we pushed our luck a bit too far on one of them.

My wife Susan wrote a text message to say that the traffic jam had made her late for her own engagement party and to request that they 'tell Keith that she loves him and Susie will be with him as soon as she can'.

It was read out on air a few minutes later, to much laughter in our car and a solemn comment from the presenter that there were 'some heartbreaking stories out there.'

The following morning, the Robin Hood Half Marathon began at ten o'clock. I was involved in the start line presentation and on the PA system introduced the clubs and individuals representing their counties in the inaugural Sweatshop/UKA Grand Prix Final. A minute before the off, my mobile phone rang. It was bound to be someone involved in the race organisation because no-one else would ring at such an inopportune moment on a Sunday morning, so I answered it.

'Is Susie there?' a voice asked.

'Eh? I think you have a wrong number.' It dawned on me as soon as I put the phone down that this was the radio station looking to do the follow up on the missed engagement party.

My mobile stayed off the rest of the morning.

✣ 98 ✣

JO FENN

I DO a lot of sit-ups each day, my absolute minimum is 300 and occasionally I'll do up to 1,000. When I go away from home for races, I maintain a superstition that I heard that Daley Thompson followed – whatever hotel number I'm given, I do that number of sit-ups between checking in and my race.

I always worry I'm going to get a high room number and that maintaining the superstition may jeopardise race prospects, so it's always an anxious time when I arrive at a hotel reception and wait for my room key.

I broke my lucky streak of matching sit ups to room number when I ran at the World Indoor Championships in Lisbon in 2001. I was given room 1426! It was my first major games and I wanted to save my energy but it didn't do me any good because I ran like a drain and was knocked out in the heats – since then I have been doing my full allocation every time and desperately hoping I don't check into anything that high again.

My other superstition is I like the number 8 in my number or to start in lane 8. It's my lucky number and if I am allocated either of those two ways then I always feel extra confident.

Beware. If I ever get number 888 and a draw for lane 8 I'll go for the world record!

✣ 99 ✣

GEOFF WIGHTMAN

AT our 2002 Puma 10k Classic road race the men's winner was a 20 year-old Tanzanian who was making his first visit to the UK. On the afternoon before the race his management team, who are the most professional in the business, sent a chaperone with him to Kings Cross, took him to his pre-booked seat on an Inter-City train service and rang me to say that he was on his way.

The race director and I met him on the platform at Wakefield station, checked him into his hotel, gave him his race number and programme, drove him around the course and then arranged a special menu and early serving of dinner for him at the race hotel.

The following morning we collected him from the hotel, drove him to the race and showed him his own personal changing and warm-up area at Dewsbury Town Hall. He proceeded to win a very exciting race, with just one second covering the first three, and also collected the cash prime award for the first to halfway. He was a popular winner and signed several autographs.

After the presentation, my colleague drove him back to the hotel for a pre-arranged late checkout enabling him to shower and change. He was then driven to Wakefield Station where my colleague, having checked that there were no problems with the London-bound services, escorted him onto his 3.30 train and rang both his management team and me to confirm that he was safely on his way.

At that point we all breathed a sigh of relief that another successful Puma 10k Classic was done and dusted. It was all over bar the magazine write-ups. Unfortunately it was to be quite a day for our Tanzanian. For reasons that are still not quite clear – possibly because he fell asleep – he got off the train at somewhere like Newark after just thirty minutes or so. We think he then realised his mistake and boarded another service but it was probably in the opposite direction. His management had given him a contact details sheet in case of emergencies but for similarly unknown reasons, he elected not to use this. His chaperone waited for him at King's Cross until after midnight. Eventually, I got a call from the police in Doncaster.

He was fine but appeared to have spent the night on Doncaster station platform until they approached him to see if he needed help. He was put onto another London train where he was met by the chaperone, a mere twenty hours after his scheduled arrival.

His request for a place in the navigation corps has since been turned down.

✤ 100 ✤
NICK PEARSON

THE staff at the Head Office of our company, Sweatshop, were reasonably fit two or three years ago. Five or six were serious runners and on their day, any one of them was capable of beating any of the others in a race. There was therefore great interest in the build-up to the Chase Corporate Challenge race in Battersea Park in July. The race distance of 3.5 miles was to everyone's liking and there was some hard training done over the preceding couple of months.

Much of the in-house speculation centred on who would be first home for the Sweatshop team. Our MD, Hugh Brasher, had got himself in good shape and was evens favourite. I went out onto the course to spectate and support my colleagues, towards the halfway point, so I didn't actually see them line up at the start.

It was therefore a considerable surprise to see Hugh when he finally came past at two miles. He was struggling. This was nothing to do with his state of fitness but was caused by his unorthodox footwear selection. He had a lightweight fluorescent Fila racing shoe on one foot and a heavy duty, high-top black leather motorcycle boot on the other. It was quite an achievement for someone whose company at that time held about £2m worth of stock, much of which comprised running shoes, to turn up with just one shoe ... and an unusual solution to try and blend the Paul Tergat and Barry Sheen influences in this one elegant ensemble.

He hobbled on in a very lopsided fashion sufficiently quickly to be approached by officials at the finish indicating that he had qualified for first place in the CEO category. He waved them away, claiming that he was ineligible but my distinct impression (he continues to deny this) is that this was to enable him to be helped through the finish funnel in order to get urgent medical attention on his feet from St John Ambulance.

✤ *101* ✤
PAULA RADCLIFFE

I WASN'T sure if I would sleep well the night before my debut in the Flora London Marathon in 2002. I had been building towards the marathon for twelve months and it had been on my mind for many of the training miles that I had covered through the winter. I had also had a week of non-stop media enquiries about how I rated my prospects. In the end I did get a pretty good night's sleep but I had some very vivid dreams and, unsurprisingly, they didn't make much sense at all.

The one I can remember most clearly still had me chuckling after I had woken up and it really had very little to do with the marathon. I dreamt that Catherina McKiernan, the 1998 Champion, was giving me a guided tour around her house in Ireland.

It was a very grand mansion, with huge rooms throughout. Inexplicably, Catherina had decorated every single surface in every single room in two-tone shades. I didn't make any comment although I was finding it very over-the-top, especially when we got to the bathroom and not only was the toilet seat a two-tone fabric but the toilet roll changed colour as we moved.

I still didn't say anything but Catherina must have detected something in my expression because she started shouting 'You don't like it do you? But, Paula , this is ART!'

The End

101 marks the end with our Paula's dream

Did you read it in one go or run out of steam?

Did you find some tales boring and not really super?

Or laugh off your fez like a new Tommy Cooper

Runners have stories, is YOURS even better?

Like that bird on *Countdown* – we're awaiting your letter

SPORT ARMAGEDDON
SPORT, MONEY, CORRUPTION, DEATH.

LENNY STEIN is a small-time cable TV station owner, based in Atlanta. For years, he has been out-bid for the television rights to major events and has to settle for homemade junk sport. He harbours big ambitions in broadcasting and decides to stage a one million dollar winner-takes-all endurance event. With no shortage of hype, 'Sport Armageddon' requires its participants to swim Lake Okeechobee in Central Florida, then cycle round the State before running from Jacksonville to Atlanta.

There are to be just five competitors – Brent Ryan of the USA, PJ Kogo of Kenya, Gaby Vaughan of Australia, Steve O'Neill of Great Britain and Leonid Karelov of Russia. All of them are supremely fit but all have crucial flaws in their characters and backgrounds. Their participation is monitored by the vindictive Stein and his hapless lieutenant Vivian Wheatley.

Many secrets emerge in the course of Sport Armageddon, including the identity of 'Zelda' the strange outsider who threatens to kill one of the competitors.

Everyone is dying to win Sport Armageddon. Somebody must win. Somebody must die ...

"Gripping ... conveys the exhaustion, mental aspects and ups and downs of a long race."

Paula Radcliffe – Double World Half-Marathon Champion

"A gripping portrayal of sports sponsorship at its very best ... or very worst."

Sebastian Coe – Double 1500m gold medallist

"...where high stakes sport meets TV survival shows and Agatha mystery. Entertaining and refreshing."

David Powell - Athletics and Triathlon Correspondent, The Times.

"Sport Armageddon has all the ingredients of a great triathlon novel."

Norman Brook – Chief Executive, British Triathlon Association

The First Four-Minute Mile and Tom Hulatt of Tibshelf

"who won the first sub-four-minute mile at Iffley Road, Oxford in 1954?" and the reply will be "Roger Bannister".

"who came second?" and a good number will reply "Chris Chataway".

"who came third?" and it is a safe bet that nobody will know.

The answer is Tom Hulatt

Tom, a mine-worker, was born and bred in the small Derbyshire village of Tibshelf near Chesterfield in 1930. He died there in 1990. He was the Derbyshire and Northern Counties One Mile champion in 1953 and 1954 and had an outstanding record as a track athlete in the midlands throughout the 1950s.

With the Iffley Road mile as a centrepiece, this book tells Tom's story. The famous race and Tom's role in it are appraised and the highlights of his careers are described.

He deserves a place in any history of one-mile running. The authors hope that this biography will secure that place for him.

With a foreword from David Moorcroft and a unique angle on the most famous event in track and field, *The First Four Minute Mile and Tom Hulatt of Tibshelf* will be a must-read for any athletics fan.

The First Four Minute Mile and Tom Hulatt of Tibshelf **is available from Descartes Publishing Limited for £7.99 + 50p p+p (UK, Eire, BFPO)**

Call 01733-343457.